To Mags
happy reading
from
Margaret

17·10·22

BY THE SAME AUTHOR

Prana Soup: An Indian Odyssey

GOOD VIBRATIONS

a Story of a Single 60s Mum

Margaret Halliday

Copyright © 2017 Margaret Halliday

The author or authors assert their moral right under the Copyright, Designs and Patents Act, 1988, to be identified as the author or authors of this work.

All Rights reserved. No part of this publication may be reproduced, copied, stored in a retrieval system, or transmitted, in any form or by any means, without the prior written consent of the copyright holder, nor be otherwise circulated in any form of binding or cover other than that in which it is published and without a similar condition being imposed on the subsequent purchaser.

To my son Sean, the star of this book

One

I woke up to a ringing in my ears. Quickly pressing the 'off' button I snuggled down under the heavy quilt and drifted back into blissful sleep. But not for long. My mind was invaded by the awfulness of waking up to another day. The small, grimy window looked out on a grey wall. Cold, ceaseless, miserable rain fell down from a heavy, listless sky. Traffic rumbled in the distance: it was Glasgow on a Monday morning awakening from its habitual weekend drunken orgy.

My feet found the threadbare rug by my bed. Sleepily I pulled on a jumper and jeans ready to face another day. Then I dashed to the bathroom which luckily was empty. The other residents of my hostel were slow to waken. They were mainly students and would later rise reluctantly for their university lectures. I was at agricultural college studying horticulture and our classes began at nine, far too early for most of us.

At breakfast the serving ladies greeted me, "Mornin' hen. Isnae it warm today? The sun may even come oot!" The eternal optimism of these people always astonished me. I hurriedly sandwiched half my scrambled egg into a spare roll for lunch. A bowl of cornflakes followed, washed down with a mug of strong tea, and then it was the bathroom again. Most of my life these last two weeks had been centred on this room, as I waited for that event which is supposed to occur once a month (so my mother told me). Crazy thoughts passed through my head. Maybe I was anaemic, or developing a terminal illness? I could not believe that anything else would cause this strange unexplained departure from regular normality. *Nothing again.* My brain was filled with an awful deadness as I packed my books for the day.

The other students were all friendly with each other, but not with me. Every coffee break I longed for it to finish. Lectures were preferable to sitting surrounded by silence, while all around me buzzed animated conversation; I sat and sweated and stared at the blank walls then huge relief swept over me when the break was over and it was time to resume work. Work was the only thing which took my mind off the dreadful nagging numbness threatening to engulf it. The day over I walked down the street, vaguely happy to have time to myself.

Back in my solitary room my thoughts drifted back to my friend Brenda's recent visit. She had come up from London to see me and sample some Glaswegian night life. She was a lively lass with long, flowing black hair, white skin and large brown eyes, which she adorned with false black eyelashes. At seventeen she had a voluptuous figure which made her very popular with boys.

She arrived one Saturday afternoon at the beginning of term, with a large suitcase. I met her at the railway station; we must have made an odd couple. I was still very much an adolescent with no figure whatever. Tall, thin and gawky with wavy, short brown hair, I tried to straighten it with cellotape, to achieve the 'Mary Quant' look, which left ugly, sticky red marks on my cheeks.

"Let's go to a disco tonight," she enthused as we walked towards the hostel.

"Great idea." I was more than willing, dying for a

chance to experience this vibrant new city's night life. "Let's leave your case in my room and then go for a hamburger and coffee. I'm starving, aren't you?"

"Sure am." We were always hungry. Sitting in the café chatting I thought how exciting it all was.

After living at home for seventeen long years I was a student in a strange city, in a strange country. An English girl, I felt I had been hurled into a rough and down to earth land. The people seemed so different. They were not so beautiful outwardly and had none of the polished poise and fashionable appearance of the average southern Englishman. Inwardly they seethed with a huge, hot friendly warmth, which spread itself all over the streets, whatever the time of day. In Glasgow you could be a total stranger but feel perfectly at home as there was always some friendly soul who would warmly smile at you in passing. Not so in the south of England where even friends might look the other way if so inclined; I'd felt a coldness there which had hurt my spirit.

Returning to reality I descended the stairs to a dull evening meal in the hostel. Stew and dumplings, followed by steamed currant pudding and lumpy custard. It was very fattening, but who was I to care about my figure, it could only expand after all. A sudden dreadful thought occurred to me. Maybe I would expand in a far more awful way than I had ever imagined? Quickly I pushed this ridiculous idea aside and went back to my room and divine remembrances.

*

After our brief expedition Brenda and I retraced our steps to the hostel. My room was my sole retreat in this strange new world which threatened to overwhelm me.

We reminisced about our school days on the south coast of England.

"Do you remember the Waves Disco we used to go to? It was right on the sea front, shaped like an ocean liner?" Brenda's big brown eyes shone with the memory.

"Yes, it was fab. The music was great but my height was a huge problem." I took a sip of coffee.

"What do you mean about your height?"

"Remember, we used to sit by the walls and the boys would parade around, checking us out before they asked us to dance."

Brenda laughed, "I know, it was like a cattle market."

"That's right! I'd try and judge their height but it wasn't easy sitting down. More than once I was mortified, because when I stood up I'd be towering over them and they just took one look and scurried away. It was *so* embarrassing."

"Hmm . . . well, I'm nearly as tall as you and it sometimes happened to me. There weren't too many tall, handsome boys around. Maybe we'll be luckier here." She flicked her hair back from her face and looked at me expectantly.

"I hope so. Oh, and those bars in the old town we went to, near the harbour, weren't they fantastic?"

"Yeah, I remember. They had low ceilings and wooden beams, with old-fashioned-looking furniture. And the cider! Do you remember the pints of rough cider? We were under-age but no-one seemed to notice."

My memories were becoming increasingly vivid.

"That stuff tasted foul. I had to drink it holding my breath it was so bad. It had a great effect though."

"It was when we got outside it hit us. We were reeling and laughing and talking to anyone we fancied. Sometimes I even went up and kissed a boy!"

"I don't remember being that daring but I remember the street lamps swinging dangerously round the post tops as I tried focusing on them. We always had to make a mad dash for the last bus home."

Brenda made a face. "That was when I started to feel sick, on the bus. Oh, and trying to sneak in when we got home without them hearing. That was the worst."

"Oh, I know. Often I had to charge straight for the loo. It was impossible to stifle it. The noise was horrendous. Of course they heard. They'd come out and give me the usual lecture, going on and on about under-age drinking and reporting me to the authorities. It was too much. I was feeling awful enough as it was. I vowed I'd never drink a drop again. I'd never have admitted that to *them* though."

"Yeah, it wasn't the best and that awful hangover the next day. I just wanted to die." Brenda's eyes were not so shiny now.

The discotheques in the resort where we lived were heaven in summer and because they were unlicensed there weren't any violent drunks. We were too young to appreciate the swarthy European boys and the trendy Englishmen. One of these latter seduced me first. I knew as soon as I saw him, one warm spring night, that he was the one. I had just left school and only vaguely knew what to expect from such an encounter. That night I was with another friend, Julie. They walked in and she spotted the man he was with, whom she knew. I had never seen them before. He was tall, taller than me. *That's a start at least,* I thought. He was dark-haired, his tight-fitting jeans and tailored shirt showing off his slim, muscular figure. His grey eyes seemed to look right into the depths of my very inexperienced self. His mouth was strong and firm, and looking back afterwards, very cruel.

They asked us to dance. The disc jockey played Diana Ross and the Supremes, *Baby Love,* while he danced with me as no-one had ever done before, pressing his strong body against mine, awakening all the latent passion that was within me. We danced several long, slow dances, making no conversation due to the volume of the music. Eventually, between dances I learnt his name, Paul, and he mine. Also I discovered he was very old, or so it seemed to me then. He was twenty-two compared to my sixteen. This age difference pleased me a great deal because most of the males at the discos were around my own age. To be dancing with someone so old, debonair and handsome I felt was a huge privilege. Towards the end of the evening they asked Julie if they could run us home. I was doubtful, but she assured me that everything would be all right, as she knew her partner quite well.

We walked out into the street and my mouth fell open with astonishment when I saw Paul's car. It was a large, black Jaguar. My immediate reaction was to absolutely refuse to travel in it. Reason told me that men who owned large cars and attempted to entice young girls into them could not be trusted. But Julie was most insistent that it was perfectly safe. More importantly we had missed the last bus, so, with a pounding heart I got into the front, whilst Paul drove. Soon Julie was being kissed passionately on the back seat, which rather upset me. The car purred along quiet roads to her house. On reaching it, he parked round the corner for fear her parents would see us.

Then he turned off the engine slowly and deliberately, his arm resting across my shoulders. Drawing me towards him his fingers caressed my neck, massaging away the nervous tension in my muscles, turning my insides into a bubbling, heaving cauldron of desire. His teeth tenderly bit into my ear lobes, his hot breath sending shivers up and down my spine. Then his firm, cool lips found mine, and I knew for sure that this was no mere boy, clumsily finding his way, but a man who knew exactly how to arouse a girl.

Julie's voice interrupted us. "I need to go now, Margaret. It's getting late."

"Okay, goodnight. See you soon," I managed to utter. She clambered out and fear enveloped me once more.

Paul turned to his friend, "Mike, you drive now." Then to me, "Let's move to the back."

The size of the back seat was a shock: we could lie along its length fully stretched out. The soft leather enveloped me and his body touched mine so closely I felt almost strangled by the sensation. At last we reached a place a couple of streets away from my house, with my virginity so far intact.

"May I see you tomorrow evening?" Paul looked hopefully at me. I was flummoxed. Why should a man like him be so desperate to see me again and so soon? Surely he had better things to do?

Stammering I replied, "I'm not sure." Nervously I straightened my clothes, wondering whether or not to take this momentous step. Eventually curiosity and desire overcame me. "All right. Would around seven do? Let's meet a long way from my place." I had to keep this secret from my mum.

"Right. Seven it is. Is down at the harbour far enough?" He looked at me with amusement.

"Yes. That's fine. See you then. Thanks for the lift." I scrambled out, keen to get away now.

I spent the next day in a fever wondering whether or not to go, and whether or not he'd be there, my mood alternating between exhilaration and dread. At last the evening arrived. Somehow I ate my tea, trying to appear normal in front of my mother.

"Where are you off to tonight?" she quizzed me. "You don't usually go out on a Sunday." I'd told her I was going out, but no details.

"Oh, I'm meeting Julie. We're just going for a walk down the harbour. It's such a nice evening." Mum didn't look too certain. It was horrible lying to her, but at least some of it was true.

I took a long bath which relaxed me slightly, washing myself in every crevice extremely carefully. Afterwards I covered my body with talc and perfume, my hands shaking with nerves. I wondered whether it was all worth it as I made up my face, carefully applying mascara and pale lipstick. I put on my shortest mini skirt and skinny top, black and white block-heeled shoes completing the picture. Finally I backcombed my hair, carefully shaping it around my face. At last I was ready and walked slowly down the road to our meeting place, my heart beating horribly. He was there waiting in his Jaguar, so cool and sure of himself. I stood trembling on the pavement, too scared to get in.

"Hi, glad you could make it. I wondered if you'd have second thoughts." He gave me a long, lingering look. I was still on the pavement.

"Well, aren't you going to get in?" He opened the front door wide. In I climbed. *It was too late to turn back now* I thought, feeling a dreadful sickness in the pit of my stomach.

"What would you like to do?"

I replied, "How about the pictures?"

"There's nothing on worth seeing." Reluctantly I agreed.

"Let's go to my place. It's not far."

This suggestion took me by surprise. I had imagined succumbing to his charms on the soft back seat of the car. Curiosity overcame me once again. I wanted to see where he lived and the prospect of a bed was a far more comfortable idea. It would also be private for how dreadful it would have been to be discovered in the car. The jag purred on its way while Paul monopolised the conversation. I was too nervous to speak.

"You know I almost didn't make it on time. Had to fix a puncture and the oil needed changing. It was such a rush."

I found myself wondering why he had gone to so much bother just to meet me, a poor, skinny young girl of just sixteen, with no figure at all. It never occurred to me that my youth and innocence alone would be sufficient temptation to any unscrupulous male. The car stopped, all too soon it seemed to me, in a street lined with large three-storey Victorian houses. I couldn't believe that he lived anywhere so large, being used to a modern bungalow myself. With great trepidation I walked up the path beside him. He opened the front door and led me up what seemed like endless flights of stairs. Sounds of great hilarity could be heard emanating from the rooms which we passed and I postulated what sort of place this could be. All sorts of imaginings raced through my brain, like the stories of white slavery which my mum had told me: a needle would be stuck in my arm at any moment. Or worse – maybe it was a brothel and I would be kept a prisoner, a prize because of my youth, having to pretend to enjoy men of all shapes and sizes from morning to night, day in, day out.

Plucking up courage I asked him, "Who do you live here with?"

"My parents and older brother," was his casual reply.

This calmed me somewhat, but I found it difficult to believe. Surely they would have been there to greet him and prevent him from taking a young girl upstairs to his room? Finally we reached the top floor and the attic which was his bedroom. It was a small, cosy room, the ceiling sloping down so low that we had to bend down. The walls were covered with pictures of naked women much to my astonished disgust. Never had I seen such images, all of which highlighted the fact that I had as yet no figure worth mentioning. I had great difficulty filling a 34A cup bra, and the sight of all those huge mammary glands staring at me did not make me feel any more at ease.

We sat down on the bed as there was nowhere else to sit. I thought this was very clever of him, for we were at once close to each other, and a bed must only mean one thing when a man and woman sit on it in such a situation. Slowly he put his arms around me and drawing me to him began to kiss me in the same divine way as before. I started to relax feeling hot inside. Then his hands gradually unbuttoned my blouse and I sat rigid wondering what he would do next. His breathing became heavier and faster as his hands expertly worked their way round my back and undid my bra. Then he caressed my stomach filling me with a sensation which I could hardly understand, never having felt like that before. He reached under my skirt, undoing my suspenders and gently stroked my thighs. My stockings were loosened, my knickers and skirt quickly following them. Impatiently I kicked off my shoes and rid myself of those cumbersome lower garments. At last I found myself naked and I lay feeling dreadfully exposed to his cold, grey eyes which travelled up and down my body, as he hurriedly undressed.

He switched off the light. *Thank goodness, he can't see me now.* Then his warm body was on top of mine. He kissed my face and neck and breathed into my ears, making me want to laugh. His fingers stroked that private place never before touched by man. I began to feel wet as his fingers gently rubbed me outside, and then very gradually eased their way up inside my hot vagina.

He whispered, "It'll be all right. I'll be very careful. Christ it's great to have a virgin. I've never had one you know."

I felt a sharp pain, and then he was inside me and I didn't feel a thing. For what seemed like an interminable time he pushed up and down on top of me. I seemed to feel far away as if I was dreaming. Suddenly he stopped and stood up, quickly catching his sperm in a handkerchief. At the time I didn't realise what a precarious precaution he had taken, but later I was appalled. I was jerked out of my dream-like state into the awful present, the horrifying thought that I might be late home uppermost in my mind. Quickly I pulled on my clothes, hastily brushing my hair. With relief I saw that it was not yet time for the last bus – I had to be home at the right time if I wanted a peaceful life.

He drove me back in silence and kissed me goodnight in an almost fatherly way, his passion now spent. There was no mention of seeing me again. Dejectedly I wandered up the road towards my place, my dreams in ashes, my new found womanhood not filling me with all the good feelings that I'd imagined it would. For months after this encounter I hoped that I would see him and I did a couple of times at the disco, or driving around in his flashy car. He never spoke or even showed the slightest sign of recognition. Gradually as the months passed the pain diminished and I thought about him less and less, until I left home to go to college in Glasgow, where I finally forgot the pain completely.

Two

After all that talking about our past Brenda and I decided to go out and find some Glaswegian night life – maybe there were good discos in this huge city, we hopefully thought. We collected a late key from the hall and set out on our exciting excursion. It was a fine night and the city lights looked bright and inviting as we walked along the street wearing our best dresses. I had bought a purple one with a silver belt that day, the hem well above the knees, it being the height of the mini skirt era.

First we went for a drink as no dancing began until after ten when the pubs shut. Following close inspection we entered a bar called The Auld House, which seemed respectable enough as many of the bars were obviously not suitable for women to enter. They were full of unshaven, uncouth old men, their pints and nips lined up beside them in preparation for the ten o'clock closing. Boldly we approached the counter. "Two half pints of beer, please," I asked confidently.

The buxom barmaid, whose dyed blonde hair showed black roots, looked suspiciously at us. "Whit kind o' beer wid yous like?"

We weren't beer drinkers and knew nothing about the various types of Scottish brew. Guessing I pointed to the nearest tap. "We'll have two halves of export."

"Coming up." The frothy liquid filled the glasses. Quickly we paid and retreated into a dark corner before she could ask any questions about our age. We sank onto the red plastic seats with relief and surveyed the scene through a haze of smoke.

"It's a bit different from home, isn't it?" Brenda sipped her beer and made a face. "This stuff tastes like piss."

"Hmm. I won't have it again," I agreed. "All the guys have pints of beer and they seem a bit drunk, don't you think?"

"Yes. Back home they only drink halves unless it's a big celebration like Christmas or a wedding. You don't often see any drunks, well not where we go, except us of course!" We both laughed.

As we settled down we began to enjoy ourselves. The atmosphere was warm and friendly, everyone chatting to each other without any embarrassment, while a group of rowdy men played darts opposite us. This was different from the pubs we knew, where friends kept themselves to themselves, only speaking to strangers when it was absolutely necessary. If anyone were to become a little outrageous as a result of a drop too much, the rest of the company would regard them with revulsion, muttering to their companions, "How dreadful, what awful behaviour, don't you think?"

Having finished our drinks we went for a coffee in a nearby Wimpy Bar. It was completely deserted except for a few giggling teenagers, the adult population still being firmly entrenched in the bars. At the magic hour of ten o'clock we wandered down the street to the discotheque which a boy at college had recommended. We surveyed the uninviting entrance, a stone alleyway with a flight of steps leading upwards at the end. However, being ever hopeful we ascended the stairs which soon ended at a red door, through which could be heard the sound of music. A large man stood barring the entrance, to stop any exceptionally drunk men from entering. He gave us a friendly look. "Guid evenin', lassies. That'll be seven shillings 'n sixpence."

This was more than we were used to paying but we grudgingly parted with our cash. Brenda hissed in my ear, "It'd better be worth it!"

The bouncer flung open the door. We went inside with mixed feelings. The disc jockey was in the centre of the room on a platform. He was playing the very best in disco music, all the latest Tamla Motown goodies which pleased us tremendously. The place was lit with flashing lights revolving around the floor and walls, making anything white glare translucently; I was secretly glad that I was wearing dark colours. In my home town I had gone to a disco wearing a white bra under a green holey jumper, and suffered agonies all night as everyone laughed at my shining bra containing my non-existent breasts. The only thing missing from the atmosphere were people. There were about half a dozen hiding at the back in the shadows. We didn't wish to join them and hurriedly went to the ladies to backcomb our hair and examine our faces for any newly developed flaws.

When we re-entered the room it was beginning to fill up and we stood expectantly surveying the scene. "Come on, let's dance," Brenda urged. I agreed, knowing that this attracted the opposite sex faster than standing at the edge of the floor, like two jellyfish stranded on the beach at low tide. Almost immediately two young men approached and asked us to dance. They looked all right and we danced energetically hoping to impress these Scottish lads with our 'with it' moves.

After we'd finished my partner asked, "Where are you from?"

"The south coast of England. I'm at college here."

"That's funny. We're from that part of the world too!"

Brenda was having a similar conversation. We signed to each other and once again headed for the toilets. "How awful! They're English too. I'm fed up with Englishmen, we need to meet some Scots," I moaned.

"You're right. Let's go back," Brenda suggested.

On our return to the floor we were relieved to see the men dancing with other girls, coldly ignoring us for having run out on them. It was not long before Brenda was asked to dance by a swarthy Italian. I was left at the edge of the floor, wondering what was going to happen next. Two boys came up and stood looking at me and laughing. I felt very tall and uncomfortable, and stood digging my nails into my hands, slouching down trying to get as low as possible, being ever conscious of my height. One of them was tall, fashionably-dressed, with a perfect profile, short, black hair and greyish-green eyes. He reminded me of my first lover but had a kinder face, which lit up with genuine merriment when he smiled. The other was also tall, but not handsome. He squinted through thick-lensed glasses and had mousey unkempt hair, a strangely misshapen pudgy nose and clothes which hung off his frame, making him look rather like a scarecrow.

I prayed that they would stop grinning and speak to me instead. Amazingly this actually happened. It is not often my prayers are answered, but that night they were with a vengeance. The consequences would be so huge and far reaching, that if I had known, I would have bolted for the door in an instant.

Over they came, both grinning from ear to ear like apes in the zoo. "Hello," they said in Glaswegian accents, accompanied by a strong smell of beery breath. *Well here goes, my first encounter with real live locals.*

"Hello," I replied, mustering up my best smile.

"Huvnae seen ya before. How do ya like it?" The handsome one asked.

"The music's great. It's my first time here." His greyish-green eyes had all my attention.

"You dinnae soond like you're frae these parts," his friend had obviously been listening.

"No, I'm from England, the south coast."

As soon as they knew I was English they became even friendlier, edging closer to get a better look. I gathered from their hilarious, though rather dubious remarks, that they thought English girls were better (or perhaps easier) game than their Scots counterparts. I was hoping that the handsome one, whose name was Steve, would ask me to dance, but instead his friend Duncan did the asking. We danced a great many fast dances until towards the end of the evening the pace slowed down, and I was in his arms smooching slowly to the music. The sensation was not altogether unpleasant. By this time Steve was dancing with a tall, beautiful blonde who had a gorgeous figure, so I resigned myself to the fact that I was stuck with Duncan. After a vast number of slow, sweaty dances we looked around for Brenda. She had disappeared, to my dismay and I imagined her getting lost somewhere in the city with her Italian dancing partner.

Duncan and I collected our coats. "Wid you like a coffee? I ken a wee place that'll be open just doon the road." I readily agreed being very thirsty after all the dancing. It was indeed a 'wee place', but there were no other customers so we sat at a corner table. Duncan took a sip of coffee and peered at me through his lenses, which made his eyes somewhat magnified. "So what brings you tae this part o' the world?"

"I'm at the Agricultural College, studying horticulture. What do you do?"

"I'm an engineer in telecommunications, a wee bit different frae horticulture. That's like gardening isnae it?" He grinned to show that he was joking. It was a sore point with me, this view that horticulture was simply gardening, but I didn't rise to the bait. I was enjoying listening to the sound of his voice, which was deep and melodious, unlike some of the more raucous accents I had heard. I changed the subject.

"Do you have any brothers and sisters?"

He looked sad. "Nae, I'm an only child. Whit aboot you?" I felt sorry for him.

"I have a sister but she's ten years older than me and I've always envied people with siblings they could play with."

"Aye, I guess I felt like that although some o' ma pals come frae big families and they're always fighting aboot something." Then we fell silent, the coffee being finished and the conversation temporarily exhausted.

"Can I run you hame?" he offered.

"I only live about five minutes walk away."

"Well, I can still gies you a lift, can't I?"

We began walking in the direction of his car. "What the hell! Look whit's happened tae ma motur!"

I looked. All his tyres were flat. "That's awful, who would do a thing like that?"

"I've got a guid idea. A so-called 'pal' wi' a weird sense o' humour. You'd better get on. It'll take me ages blowing all these up."

"Okay. I'm really sorry. Hope you get home all right." I began heading up the road.

He shouted after me, "See you there next week, maybe?"

"Probably I'll be there. 'Bye." I trudged back to the hostel feeling strangely happy and content, thinking what a pleasant evening it had been, at the same time worrying about the whereabouts of Brenda.

I was getting ready for bed when there was a knock at my door. Brenda came in looking distraught. She sat down on my bed running her fingers through her now tangled hair, her face white. I looked at her with concern. "What happened to you?"

"I went back to Giovanni's flat. He was so gorgeous, I couldn't resist."

"What a crazy thing to do!"

"I know that now. God, his flat was in some mess. It was filthy and smelt foul. There were dirty dishes lying everywhere. The only piece of furniture was an unmade bed in the centre of the room."

"It sounds ghastly. What did you do?"

"Well, we sat on the bed cos it was the only place and had a cigarette. He didn't have any. I had to give him one. Then he started trying to take off my clothes.

Somehow I managed to fight him off. I don't know where I got the strength! He might have a black eye or two. I got away but I left my lighter behind."

"I wouldn't worry about it. You're lucky you weren't raped or even murdered, going back to a stranger's flat, and a foreigner at that."

"But it was a really expensive lighter. My last boyfriend gave it to me for Christmas. I wish I could remember where his place was. It's too bad."

"Oh shut up and go to bed," I was losing patience. The excitement of the evening was catching up with me. Eventually she left and I was soon asleep.

Three

The next morning arrived all too quickly. We both overslept, missing breakfast, which was between the unearthly hours of eight to eight thirty. Most Sundays I managed to stagger down the stairs, often sitting in total solitude, the rest of the inhabitants not being so bothered about their stomachs. After hurriedly eating I then went back to bed to fall asleep again immediately.

When I finally did surface that morning I realised there was only an hour to go before Brenda's train left for London. Quickly I pulled on my clothes and rushed to her door. Knocking loudly I yelled, "Brenda, hurry up and get up or you'll miss your train."

"Oh no!" she opened the door and let me in. At breakneck speed we both crammed her belongings into her case. We almost ran to the station down deserted streets, strewn with the previous night's chip wrappings, empty beer cans and whisky bottles. The morning was surprisingly bright and clear for November. It cheered us up and remembering everything that had happened the night before, I felt like singing and dancing along the way.

We arrived at the station with time for a quick coffee and a roll in the buffet. Immediately we regretted entering. The prices were ridiculously high, the coffee weak and warm and the roll had a microscopic amount of butter on it. The beige plastic tables and chairs bore the stains and marks of past travellers and the whole place had a thoroughly dismal air, the red tomato-shaped sauce containers the only spots of brightness.

We finished our breakfast, grim though it was and hurried to the platform. The train was already there. "Bye, Margaret. Thanks for the great time."

"Promise you'll write soon. I'll see you in the Christmas holidays when I'm home. It won't be long."

Slowly the train disappeared from view, her waving arm getting smaller and smaller. Once more I was all alone in that big city but full of hope that things would get more exciting. I vowed to study devoutly every night of the week for the end of term exams, leaving the weekend free for gallivanting.

*

The week passed quickly enough, as large quantities of work were piled upon me from college. I kept to the strict routine of studying every evening, only occasionally letting my mind wander back to Saturday night, wondering what the next one would have in store. Saturday morning dawned, damp but dry and I went window shopping to pass the time.

Back at the hostel I slowly ate my tea, knowing that the evening would be long. I had to wait until ten to venture out, having no friend this time to go for a drink or coffee with before the disco. After my meal I had a sleep, more to pass the time than anything else. Then I had a long bath, most of the hostel inhabitants having departed to the pictures or parties much earlier. I spent a great deal of time getting dressed, deciding on a pink mini skirt with a geometric design, accompanied by a skimpy black polo neck jumper and black tights. I splashed liberal quantities of perfume on my upper body, applied thick black mascara to my eyelashes, with pale lipstick and powder completing the picture. At last it was time to leave and I went downstairs, feeling rather embarrassed about going out so late. Furtively I took a late key and let myself quietly out of the big, heavy front door.

I rushed down the road through the pouring rain, clutching an umbrella, wearing a PVC mac, my feet becoming cold and wet in my black and white block-heeled shoes. The doorman let me in with no sign of recognition. I headed straight for the toilet as there were few people present. In my haste to leave the hostel at a respectable hour I'd arrived too early. Two girls stood tidying their hair. They turned to me smiling. "Hi. What awful rain that is. My hair's soaking," the younger-looking of the two exclaimed.

"It certainly is. I was glad of my umbrella but my feet are sodden."

"Are you on your own?" The older one kindly enquired.

"Yes, I am. Last week I came with my girlfriend who was visiting from London. We had a great time but she's gone now and I don't have anyone to come with."

"Oh, that's too bad. You can stay with us if you want. I'm Adelina and this is my younger sister, Maria. We were born here but our parents are Italian. We wish they'd stayed in Italy for the sunshine."

That explained their dark looks, I thought. They were both beautiful, with olive skins, long, black wavy hair and brown eyes. "That's very kind of you. I'm Margaret and I'm new here. I just started college and live in the YWCA hostel up the road."

"We both work in offices and still live with our parents, worse luck," Adelina moaned.

Maria added, "Yeah, we don't earn enough money to escape. We're looking for a couple of rich guys to release us!"

"And you reckon you'll find them here?" I laughed and they joined in. It felt good to be chatting and I realised I'd hardly spoken to a soul all day.

"Come on, let's go and dance," they urged me out into the room. More folk had arrived and some were dancing to the fast music. I looked around but there was no sign of the two boys who had not been far from my thoughts all week. I wasn't too bothered as now I had my new friends to talk to. Soon three boys came up and asked us to dance, which we did, gyrating to the beat of the latest Beatles hit.

We had finished dancing and were leaning against the wall, regaining our breath, when in walked the two boys I most wanted to see. My heart turned over and I felt a thrill run up and down my body centring on my abdomen, making it feel hot and quivery. They saw me at once and came over, both looking extremely pleased to see me. It was a huge relief, as I had suffered agonies thinking that they might ignore me completely when we next met.

"Hi, Margaret. It's guid tae see you. Who're your pals?" Duncan seemed nicer-looking than before.

"Oh, we just met in the ladies, but I guess we're pals by now."

"Och, that's great. Let's huv a dance." Steve had disappeared into the back recesses of the room, leaving me to his friend.

We danced and danced until exhaustion finally overcame us, when we flopped down thankfully on the black plastic seats which lined the walls. It was dark around the seats, the flashing lights centred on the dance floor, cascading with their multi-coloured hues over the writhing, rhythmically rotating bodies. Breathlessly we leant against each other, inhaling our clean, hot sweat mingling with the odours of perfume and after-shave. Slowly his arms surrounded me, pulling me closer. He began breathing into my hair, covering my face with soft kisses. Then he started kissing my lips passionately, drawing his rough tongue over my teeth, his saliva mingling with mine, making me feel damp and excited.

"Come on, let's get oot o' here," Duncan breathed in my ear. I agreed. If we had gone on any longer we would have made a complete spectacle of ourselves. We gathered up our coats and made for the exit. We descended the stairs none too steadily, drunk from our passion until the cold air suddenly hit us, jerking our numbed senses back to reality. "Wow, it's baltic oot here," he hugged me to him, then continued, "Dae you fancy meeting up the morra night?" I wasn't expecting this; Sunday was such a dead day, the chance to brighten it up enticing.

"That'd be great."

"Okay, see you the morra then, aboot seven? I'll pick you up ootside the hostel."

Too shy to ask where he planned to take me I readily agreed. "I'd better gang and check the motur. Dinnae want a repeat o' last week's fun." He kissed me goodbye disappearing down the street.

I wandered up the road, trying to stop the urge to leap

about and sing at the top of my voice. It felt as if I was gliding along on a cushion of air, not noticing the cold, as I was burning all over remembering those recent caresses and the anticipation of more to come. Happily I let myself into the hostel and sank into a sound sleep almost immediately.

*

The following night came. I waited expectantly in the front lounge which overlooked the busy street, having spent a couple of happy hours preparing for this big event, feeling clean and sexy. He arrived only five minutes late, but that had seemed like a lifetime as I nervously waited, a sick sensation in the pit of my stomach. As soon as I saw him all the agitation ceased and I rushed out to the car.

He flung open the door of his dark-blue Ford Anglia, grinning widely, "It's yersel so it is. Quick, jump in afore the wardens catch us."

Once inside he immediately drove away. "So, was the car all right? No more flat tyres?"

"Nae, thank goodness. I'd foond oot who'd done it and gave him hell. I dinnae think he'll dae it again in a hurry."

There wasn't much traffic and we quickly left the city centre behind. After our initial outburst silence reigned inside the car, neither of us being confident enough to begin a conversation. I was content to surrender to the warm upholstered car seat and the soft throbbing of the engine, finding the silence between us pleasantly soothing.

As we gathered speed he said, "I stay oot this way. I thought we'd go tae ma local for a drink, if you like?"

"Yes, that sounds fine. Which direction are we going in?"

"North west. This is the main route oot tae Loch Lomond and the west coast. It's beautiful up there, moontains 'n lochs an' all that. Maybe I'll tak' you some time."

"I'd like that. My mum took me to the Isle of Skye. It was wonderful except for the rain and midges."

"Och aye, those wee beasties are a menace right enough."

"My sister, Jean, stays near Inverness, at Culloden. There's no midges there."

"Culloden, where yous lot defeated us!" Duncan turned to smile at me.

"Don't blame me! I'm not really English. My dad's mum was pure Scottish from Fife." I was proud of my Scottish ancestry.

"Och well, that's all right then." He settled down to driving in silence again. I'd been gazing out the window at the outskirts of the immense city which never seemed to end, just streets and streets of high old red sandstone tenements, some built on steep slopes. Then we came to wider, more open avenues lined with post war bungalows, with large, carefully kept gardens and double garages. At last we were free of the city. Cows and sheep grazed in green fields bordered by trees with gently rolling hills behind. I realised how much I'd missed the country with its smell of damp earth, never having been far away from it before.

We arrived at his local, which was a fine, old hotel with wooden beams and brasses hanging on the walls. There were no Sunday licences for pubs in the sixties.

Beer glasses dangled with glinting grandeur around the bar, just waiting to be taken down and filled with the brown foaming brew.

Duncan led the way to the bar. "Can I get you a drink?" Remembering my previous experience with export I asked for a Bacardi and coke, my usual tipple when not drinking rough cider. "There's a seat ower there, in the corner by the fire. I'll bring them ower." Obediently I sat down and gazed into the glowing coals. It was lovely and cosy and I took off my coat and cardigan. Duncan stood chatting at the bar to an older man. Occasionally they glanced in my direction. He came and placed the glasses on the table and we sipped our drinks (or should that be I sipped and he gulped – franticly!)

"Who was that guy you were talking to?" I was determined to make conversation even if it meant embarrassing him.

"Och, that's auld Jock. He's always here propping up the bar n' blethering."

"It looked like you were gossiping about me."

"Dinnae worry. He just wanted to ken who you are. I telt him nice things aboot you."

"Such as. . ?" The Bacardi was giving me some courage. He took several gulps of beer before replying.

"Och, ye ken. Just whit you've telt me, aboot being frae England and at college. That's all."

Ah, well. So much for fishing for compliments. The rest of the evening passed pleasantly. We got to know more about our families and interests. He was a roadie with a band, but wasn't at all musical – it was the technical side of it he enjoyed.

At closing time, having finished our drinks, he sheepishly suggested going for a drive, which we did, despite my inner feelings of alarm. He didn't drive far, stopping at the edge of a quiet road which was lined with tall pine trees. He switched off the engine and rested his arm across my shoulders. As he was kissing me I kept imagining people peering through the windows, and although this was unnerving, it also made me very excited, a wonderful itchy feeling beginning to pulsate in my lower regions.

Then he suggested, "Let's move tae the back for some mair room or the gear stick's gonna cause me an injury." I agreed but I was wondering when I should broach the subject of contraception, having only been in that situation once before and then being too scared to mention it. However, as his kisses became increasingly passionate and his hands began to explore my hot, aching body, I kept putting off the awkward question, thinking that it would upset him and spoil the whole evening. Finally I decided not to mention it at all and curiosity getting the better of me, I carefully unzipped him, incredulously feeling the long, cool hardness of his erect penis. For several minutes my hands stroked up and down the full length of his shaft. Then he could control himself no longer, knelt in front of me on the hard car floor, grabbed my buttocks and entered my hot, throbbing vagina which had been lubricated copiously, causing no pain at all. He moved slowly at first, then began to pump in and out at a furious pace, breathing heavily all over me. At this I became very alarmed, realising that soon his sperm would spurt up inside me, so I vigorously thrust my posterior backwards, causing him to be quickly removed, not a moment too soon as he came in huge spurts all over the floor and seat.

Neither of us spoke and he showed no sign of resentment at my action, so I assumed he'd realised why I'd behaved in that way. With relief I remained silent, snuggling close to him as he reclined on the seat. We must have dozed off because suddenly we were aware of being cold and cramped. Hurriedly we pulled on our bottom clothing: it had been too cold to undress completely.

At last he broke the silence, "It's getting late. I'd better take you hame. Have to gae tae work the morra, worse luck." Sleepily we clambered onto the front seats and he drove away to the strains of the Supremes, *'You can't hurry love'* on the radio.

He enjoyed driving, especially at night and sped recklessly along the roads intent on overtaking as many other drivers as possible. I relaxed damp and exhausted at his side, vaguely watching the constant mad race against these unknown drivers hurtling along in their boxes on wheels. The stars shone coldly in the dark sky and I was once again overcome with a sensation of peaceful, warm contentment. He stopped outside the hostel and gingerly kissed me goodnight, a sudden shyness enveloping us. "Will you be goin' tae the dancin' on Friday?" he asked, " cos if you are I could meet you there." I mumbled that I'd probably go, feeling rather disappointed with this tentative arrangement.

Four

The week seemed interminably long, filled only with day after day at college, and night after night of studying such fascinating subjects as accounting and engineering. It was relieved only by my favourite – pestology. There was a certain satisfaction in learning about the habits of mites and the multitudinous diseases which they caused, oblivious of the chaos which this brought upon the agricultural community. They were especially attractive to draw, with their many jointed hairy legs, huge bristles sticking out all over their fat, round little bodies.

Finally Friday night arrived. In order to survive the long drawn out evening and to give me courage, in case he shouldn't be there, I purchased a bottle of strong cider on the way home. After eating my lonely tea, I made my way up to my little room. Then I had a long, hot soak in the large bath in the white tiled bathroom opposite. Sitting on my bed, wrapped in a fluffy towel, I began to sip the cider. The sweet, rough taste made me recoil at the first few mouthfuls until I began to enjoy it. I finished the bottle feeling rather peculiar, finding it awkward to dress and attempt to apply make-up. In the end I was ready and unsteadily made my way down the stairs, hastily collecting a late key before anyone noticed my drunken state, then out the front door. The cold air hit me, instantly bringing me to my senses. I strode briskly down the street, confidently strutting up the steps of the club, making an instant beeline for the ladies. I hazily regarded myself in the mirror, feeling ridiculously pleased, then spent a long time sitting ruminating upon life, perched on the toilet. At length I gathered myself together sufficiently to reach the dance floor, where Duncan immediately pounced on me.

He instantly ascertained the state I was in. "Whit have you been drinking? You look blootered."

"Oh, Duncan, I had a bottle of cider. It was too strong. Let's dance." I draped myself over him and attempted to sway to the music.

"Och, Margaret, this isnae working, you're all ower the place. Let's get oot o' here." He took my arm and escorted me out to his car. "Get in. We'll gae for a drive and maybe you'll feel better." Being in no fit state to argue I got in. As soon as the car began to move, my stomach began to move in sympathetic rhythm, filling me with nausea. Hurriedly winding the window down I vomited the entire contents of my stomach out, the wind blowing them dramatically along the length of the car. Afterwards I felt enormously better, vowing to never partake of strong cider again.

He drove out into the country, eventually stopping in an isolated field at the end of a track. He began to kiss me, but I broke away. "Oh, I must smell foul. My mouth tastes of sick. How can you kiss me?"

"Your breath smells sweet, honest," he breathed into my ear. With that I surrendered, first to his lips and then his penis, all restraint fleeing, the alcohol having deadened my alarm centres. We came together several times, his hot sperm shooting up inside me, filling me with ecstasy. Our passion spent, he kissed me tenderly as we lay curled up together, but never a word was spoken about what we had just experienced, although I wanted to discuss it. Adolescent embarrassment kept us tongue-tied. He drove quietly back and invited me to go for a drink the following night. I readily agreed, then collapsed into bed contentedly exhausted.

These meetings continued until just before the Christmas vacation, when the monthly dread of missing my period began to increasingly become a reality. I was in a panic about what to do during my constant visits to the bathroom. I had read novels and seen films in which women in trouble had gathered together all their savings, wretchedly creeping to a back street abortionist to end their misery. This generally happened in some dark, dirty room, the abortionist rapidly disappearing into the murky darkness, clutching a bundle of notes greedily to her chest, her raincoat pulled up over her ears to disguise her from inquisitive passers-by. Back in the room the victim would lie for ages, staring vacantly into space, eventually rousing herself to return to the world. Others, not so fortunate, would perish at the hands of these butchers, finding a different kind of release.

My mind was assailed by similar thoughts, becoming more and more exaggerated and grotesque in my fevered imagination. I had a hundred pounds saved from my previous year's employment in the park back home, where I'd done my pre-college practical training. This I hoped would be sufficient payment for one of these ghastly operators.

I'll have to find a doctor, I thought, but how in this big city? Night after night I walked the streets looking for doctors' signs in the grimmest areas, hoping that they would admit me and put an end to the agony of my mind. I soon realised that I was being stupid. The obvious place to ask for help was at college. Tentatively

I approached the receptionist, "I was wondering if you could help me?"

"Of course. What's the problem?"

"Do you know how I might find a doctor?" My face burned with shame but she seemed not to notice.

"Yes, that's easy. There are lists of doctors at the Post Office," she replied helpfully.

"Oh, thank you." I quickly retreated in case she asked any questions. *Why didn't I think of that? I'm so daft*, I rebuked myself.

At the end of class I scuttled off to the Post Office and was given a large, black book filled with names and addresses. I chose a female doctor who had a practice some distance away. After a long and wearisome bus ride I reached the street. It looked sufficiently tatty to fit my fantasies of back street abortionists. I entered the surgery full of trepidation, my heart thumping painfully against my ribs. Hard brown leather seats lined the walls of the bare waiting room, which was devoid of anything to relieve the gloom. A few medical posters were stuck on the dirty cream walls, advertising the merits of having a TB jab and other health matters. I chose a seat in the far corner and tried not to look at the other patients. They all sat rigidly, occasionally bursting into raucous coughing, blowing their noses on large grey handkerchiefs, or morosely turning the pages of a crumpled magazine. I chose one and hid behind it, barely able to absorb anything. After what seemed an interminable wait I was summoned into the doctor's room.

"Good afternoon. How are you?" she did not wait for a reply, "please sit down." She established that I was a temporary resident and the relevant forms were completed, making me feel threatened by bureaucracy. Placing her pen carefully on the table she asked, "So, what can I do for you?"

Suppressing the urge to shout, "Give me an abortion!" I nervously explained that my period was fourteen days overdue.

She calmly replied, "Well, this is quite normal for girls of your age. There's nothing to worry . . ."

I interrupted excitedly, "I think I might be pregnant." I was surprised the doctor showed no sign of shock.

"I see," she began to write, "I'll give you a prescription for some tablets which should bring on menstruation. If this doesn't happen, please come back and see me."

Thankfully I retreated, clutching the prescription which I hoped was for magic pills that would painlessly cause the obstacle to be removed. I went in search of the nearest chemist and waited impatiently. Back in my room I hastily took the first tablet, then sat around waiting for something to happen. I soon became bored and went to have my tea, which I enjoyed for the first time in two weeks.

I was to take one pill for three consecutive days, which I did, constantly hoping for something to happen. The three days passed, and the fourth. I began to despair. The weekend came round again, and the fifth day. I was supposed to be meeting Duncan that night and resigned myself to telling him of my predicament, hoping that he'd be able to help, exactly how I wasn't too sure. Certainly I did not want a child right at the start of my career at the tender age of seventeen. The idea of marriage crossed my mind as a romantic thing to do, until the harsh reality of our situation hit me.

Neither of us had much money and we were both too young to settle down. It would be a disaster.

I slept in, missing breakfast and mooned around the rest of the morning feeling miserable. Then I began to have pains in my abdomen. Could this be it? Hopefully I went to the bathroom where I nearly shouted for joy! Now I was convinced the pills were magic.

When I went out to Duncan's car I was radiant, but never mentioned the reason. "Hi, Margaret. You look great! Dae you fancy coming tae ma place? Ma folks are oot the night." *Oh dear, I should tell him about my condition, but it's so embarrassing. I'll just have to go.* He lived in the suburbs, near where we'd gone for a drink. We came to a quiet street and he stopped outside an impressive detached bungalow which was surrounded by a mature garden with large trees and bushes. Inside it was comfortable and homely. We settled down in front of a roaring coal fire, which was the height of luxury after all our cold, uncomfortable nights on the back of the car. After a great deal of passionate kissing and tentative exploration, I had to tell him the 'bad news', without mentioning my previous fears of pregnancy. "Och, that's okay. Wid you like a coffee?"

"Yes. That'd be great," I replied, with a sigh of relief. He brought in two large steaming mugs which calmed us down. Then we had to leave before his parents returned, carefully tidying the room and washing the mugs.

"Will I see you at the club next Friday?" he asked outside the hostel.

"Yes," I responded and waved as he drove away.

I was in for a rude awakening at the club. He was

waiting outside. "Hi there, Margaret. I must talk tae you. Let's walk." He began walking up the road towards my hostel. "I dinnae want tae dae this, but we've got tae stop seeing each other or you'll fall pregnant." *Oh, he had been concerned so why hadn't he used condoms in that case?* Miserably I agreed. He looked sadly at me, "The Christmas holidays'll soon be starting 'n you'll be off hame, forgetting all aboot me." At that moment I could not believe this but was too shocked to say anything. We parted without a hug or kiss, the damp night air blowing cruelly around us. I cried myself to sleep, surprised by my emotions, only then fully realising what he meant to me.

Five

In the light of a new day things didn't seem as bad. I hoped he'd miss me and we'd be reunited in the New Year. There was also a man, Edwin, in my home town who I'd been infatuated with the previous summer. I had met him through my job as a horticultural trainee in the local park. My presence caused quite a sensation as I was the first female to be employed there since the land army girls in the war. The local press came and took a photo of me standing in a bed of scarlet salvias, collecting seed in a trug: it was a large picture and graced the front page.

During the long winter there was little outside work to be done. The exception was the raking up of piles upon piles of leaves from the many large trees, including oak, beech and chestnut. By the time we had finished it was spring when the flower beds could be prepared. When I was out raking I was indistinguishable from the rest of the men, being clad in jeans, boots and a duffel coat, my short brown hair hidden under a woolly hat. The gang paused many times during the day to roll up their cigarettes, which dangled from their weather beaten lips while they pulled wide, wooden rakes through masses of damp leaves. When it began to rain we would stand huddled together under a tree with sufficient leaves left on it to shield us from the cold, wet drops. They would go to great trouble to find a tree out of sight of the path, where the foreman would be searching to bring us into the potting sheds. Here we would be given tasks, such as washing and disinfecting flower pots, which no-one enjoyed.

The older men had a vast stock of tales to tell about past employees. One of their favourites concerned a young lad who was keen on gathering shiny, red conkers, which fell from the chestnut trees. A beautiful autumnal day dawned and they decided to play a trick on him. Harold, a short, fat man, with a wide face and mischievous grin, related: "I told him, hey, young Mick, there's an absolutely enormous, perfect conker under that pile of leaves. Next thing he thrust his bare hand into the centre of the pile. It was so funny! His expression changed from delight to disgust as he slowly withdrew his hand. Guess why?" he didn't wait for a reply, "it was covered in dog's dirt!" Having finished recounting this tale, all of them guffawed with laughter. Although I joined in, secretly I was rather concerned in case they decided to play an even nastier trick on me.

Indeed, my turn came in the spring when we were scything the long grass up the steep banks in the wild part of the park. As we swung our curved steels through the blades of grass frogs would leap up, and now and then one would meet a sorry end, sliced by the cruel blade. Many lost a leg and squirmed about in agony. This horrified me although I was none too fond of these amphibious creatures. Every time I spotted a frog, either whole or in pieces, I made a great deal of fuss which the men found most amusing. One day I felt too warm and hung my duffel coat from the branch of a tree. I overheard a couple of guys passing by remark, "Is that a girl cutting the grass up there?"

His friend peered in my direction. "It's a boy, of course. I've never seen a female working here."

This exchange did not amuse me. My breasts, although small, were visible and I was very conscious of their size. In fact, on the removal of my outer layer one of the older men, who was about on a level with my bust, prodded one breast with his forefinger and remarked with a wipe of his nose, "Ah, they're real! Thought you didn't have any, always covered up in your duffel." I felt embarrassed and humiliated by this. There was worse to come.

Lunchtime came. I lifted down my coat and put it on. As we walked along the path the men kept glancing at me and sniggering. "What's the matter with you lot?" I queried, still smarting from the previous exchange. We were nearing the shed where we ate our sandwiches and brewed tea, when they all broke into gales of laughter.

I stopped, baffled by their merriment, until Harold managed to gasp, "Look at your pocket. I think you've got something in it!" I looked down. To my alarm my eyes met the beady gaze of an enormous toad. He was so large he was completely wedged in, unable to move.

I stood still, frozen with fright and shouted hysterically, "Oh, you horrible men. Take it away, get rid of it, please!" They all hung around making the most of my predicament, pointing and guffawing loudly. This would be a fine tale to tell. At last one of the kinder men, a leanly handsome Pole, called Stefan, removed my coat and shook the poor beast out of its pocket. It hopped away, as relieved as I was to be free. That was the only really nasty trick they played on me, but I shall never forget the horror of it.

In the spring a number of new employees arrived. They'd been recruited from the labour exchange and were a weird bunch, all intent on evading work. Most of the day they lent upon their tools, attempting to perform the minimum of digging, hoeing or weeding. They only became active when the figure of the foreman came into view, striding purposefully towards them puffing at his pipe.

One of these newcomers was strangely attractive, but he disturbed me so much that initially I tried to stay away from him. He was tanned with thinning blonde hair and loped around rather like a degenerate chimpanzee, his back being rather bent. At every available opportunity he attempted to engage me in conversation. I learned that he was single and lived alone in a room full of his paintings. He came from a fisher family, but preferred to paint as fishing was too hard a job for him with his bad back. Bob Dylan was his hero and he tried to emulate both his singing and appearance. As I worked I could hear him warbling plaintively:

"I ain't gonna work on Maggie's farm no more. No, I ain't gonna work on Maggie's farm no more." Apparently he also played the guitar and I was curious to hear this as his singing was quite good.

Spring lengthened into summer and he began asking, "Maggie, why don't you come up to my place and see my paintings? We could have a coffee or a beer and I'd serenade you with my guitar." I kept refusing, but my heart would pound with excitement during each approach. One day I was returning from lunch when I noticed the potting shed wall. Written in chalk, in large letters for all to see was: *'Margaret, please come up and see my etchings tonight at seven thirty'.* After this he'd written his name, Edwin, and address. I was mortified. The men made lewd jokes about it all afternoon, driving me to distraction. I kept denying that I was going to accept his invitation but as I walked out of the gate homewards that night, he appeared astride his rickety old bike.

"Well, Maggie, are you going to come tonight?" He looked at me expectantly, his eyes creasing into a smile. I felt my will falter, my heart beating wildly.

"Okay, I'll come," I spluttered breathlessly. I wasn't certain that I'd have the courage to actually go, being unsure about his intentions. He cycled off shouting and cheering at the top of his voice, so great was his jubilation.

*

At the appointed hour I found myself hot and flustered knocking at his door. "Come in, Margaret. So glad you made it." He looked clean and fresh – much more presentable than when he was at work. "Sit down and make yourself at home," he said, clearing a space on the settee. "A lot of this mess is my flatmate Mel's. He's out at his girlfriend's tonight, thank goodness." The walls were covered with paintings. Some looked like self portraits while others were vividly coloured abstracts – not at all to my taste. "What do you think of my etchings then?" He regarded me quizzically, his head on one side. I put on what I hoped was an earnest, artistic look.

"They're intriguing. Is that you in those ones over there?"

"Yes, in all my moods. It's a kind of therapy for me painting them."

I pointed at a particularly angry-looking one. "I wouldn't want to be around when you felt like that. It's quite scary."

"Yeah, it frightened me a bit, but don't worry I'm

okay now. Would you like to hear my guitar?" I said 'Yes' and hoped his playing would be better than his painting. He sat cross-legged on the floor and lovingly caressed his guitar resting across his knees. He began to play and croon Dylan, *"All I really want to do is, baby, be friends with you."* I sat uneasily on the edge of the settee, and after what seemed an interminably long time of his whining and strumming he stopped and offered me a coffee. While he was busy in the kitchen I relaxed a little and wondered what would happen next. Part of me was relieved that he hadn't made a move, but another part was panting in dreaded anticipation.

He came back carrying two steaming mugs of coffee and sat next to me. Placing them on a table he proceeded to announce, "You know, Maggie, I fought in the second World War and during the fighting a terrible thing happened: I lost my vital parts, know what I mean?" He was watching my shocked face closely. "'Course this means that I can't function sexually, you understand?" My naively young head was reeling. It couldn't be true. He wasn't old enough, was he? No, of course he wasn't. But then why tell me this ghastly story?

"Edwin, I don't believe you. You're too young to have fought in the war, but I guess maybe you've been injured down below?" He began to laugh uproariously and I felt extremely confused.

"Oh, Margaret, you're so gullible! How could you believe anything like that?" Then he leant over and began kissing me extremely sensuously, which took me completely by surprise. I was still reeling from his kisses as he removed my skirt and pants. He attempted to insert his finger but had no success as I was totally turned off by his antics. Next he leapt off the settee and ran into the kitchen returning with a rather grimy milk bottle. I was rooted to the seat, my bottom half still naked. He stood holding the bottle threateningly before me. "It'd do you the world of good to have this shoved up you!" I began to panic, scrabbling for my pants thinking that he must be insane. Then he once again went into fits of laughter. He put the bottle down, placed his arms around me and whispered in my ear, "Don't be so stupid." He began to kiss my face and neck and I started to relax. He stood up and removed his trousers and pants. To my relief I saw that he had all the correct parts. We moved onto his double bed and rolled, romped and rollicked for some time. But it was useless. Neither of us were in the mood after all his clowning and my hysteria. There was no time to return to his flat again before I went to Glasgow, but we made an arrangement to meet during my Christmas holidays from college.

Six

The holidays arrived and I boarded the London train from Glasgow with mixed feelings. I was looking forward to the break and seeing my friends, but also wondering what would happen on my return. Before going home, I'd arranged to stay with Brenda in north London the week before Christmas as her family had moved there. She met me in the evening at the station, where I left my luggage.

"It's great to see you again, Margaret. Do you fancy going for something to eat?" I was starving as usual.

"It's good to see you too. Do you know anywhere near here that's cheap?" She led the way to a small café which served tasty snacks. We caught up with our news and I told her about Duncan.

"Oh, Margaret. That's too bad. Maybe you'll get back together. You can take precautions, you know." She gazed at me earnestly, flicking her long, black hair away from her face.

"Yeah, well I've heard of condoms, but I'm too embarrassed to mention them, and I'd die if I had to buy any."

"There are clinics you can go to, special ones for unmarried girls. They could prescribe you the birth control pill." This was a very new development and I'd heard nothing about it.

"I wouldn't know how to find one of those clinics in

Glasgow – that's if they've got them. Is this pill safe?"

"I think it is, but I'm not taking it myself. I've just heard about it." I sat worriedly chewing my fingernails.

"Hey, come on! We're on holiday. It's time to party. I know a fabulous all night discotheque which'll be opening soon. Let's go!" She got up, quickly pulling on her coat. I wasn't really in the mood but didn't want to disappoint her.

When we reached the disco the doorman took my Scottish pound note entrance fee with great suspicion. "You know young lady, that this is only worth nineteen shillings and sixpence." I gave him my best smile and he grudgingly let me pass. Inside was an enormous room full of young people dancing, jiving or just making up their own moves. We sat down in a corner but it wasn't long before two young men asked us to dance. They told us that they lived locally and often came there.

After one dance Brenda's partner informed us,"It's not done to sit down in here. You have to dance all night!" We both started laughing.

"But that'd be impossible," I exclaimed. We soon realised that they were entirely serious, so we danced on and on and on. As the hours passed I simply stood still, occasionally wiggling my posterior to show that I was still conscious. The black teenagers in particular never seemed to tire and kept in beautiful rhythm with the music, filling me with envy of their sensuous movements.

About five in the morning we could take no more, and escorted by our faithful dance partners we limped exhaustedly out onto the street. We walked painfully to the train station, our feet being covered in blisters. We tried swapping shoes which was worse and eventually resorted to our stockinged feet, hanging on limply to the boys, who seemed unaffected by our dance marathon. They kept our spirits up, cracking jokes continuously. Without their support we would probably have collapsed. Finally we came to the station and said 'goodbye' to our gallant companions. We sank down on a wooden bench waiting for the early train. We managed to stay awake for the short journey and at length staggered into Brenda's house and the blissful comfort of bed, where we slept soundly until lunchtime.

    I went downstairs and found my friend telling her parents about our night. Her mother laughed and said, "You must be mad, the pair of you. Come and sit down, Margaret. I've cooked a full English breakfast for you both." We were ravenous and ate everything she put before us. What a great Mum!

    That week I worked on sorting and delivering the Christmas post, which had the simultaneous effect of hardening my blisters and supplying me with much needed cash for the holiday. At the end of the week we both departed to my home on the south coast to spend Christmas. Brenda was keen to catch up with all her old friends and was going to stay with her aunt and cousins. I'd arranged to meet Edwin the day before I was due home, and decided he wouldn't mind me turning up with Brenda.

    Edwin opened his door wide, "Welcome girls. Come on in out of the cold," he smiled, his eyes travelling up and down Brenda, only giving me a cursory glance. "Make yourselves comfortable," he offered, pointing towards the settee, which was extremely tidy like the rest of the room, his paintings stacked in a corner. "Would you like a glass of bubbly to celebrate

Christmas?" We sat sipping our drinks, regarding him with interest. He'd made a lot of effort with his appearance: clean shaven, hair combed back neatly, freshly laundered checked shirt and pressed jeans. He began questioning Brenda about her background, her likes and dislikes, her future plans, all the time maintaining eye contact. I sat impatiently, wondering if he were ever going to speak with me and regretted bringing her. Finally he turned to me and remarked, "You shouldn't have brought such an attractive friend with you, Margaret. Why, she's got twice as much flesh on her bones than you, twice as cuddly!"

I sat stunned by his outburst, never having dreamed that he would make advances to Brenda – he was *my* 'property'. I hoped for an objection from her, but she sat impassively as if nothing were wrong. I felt like crying and headed for the bathroom to recover. On my return they were sitting together in deep conversation. He then delivered another blow, "We think it's best if you sleep in my mate's room. He's away for Christmas and won't mind." Shocked, I thought *he won't mind but* I *do,* and glared at both of them. I was too hurt to cause a scene and slunk down the corridor to the other room. It was very cold so I crawled into bed fully clothed, pulling the freezing sheets up around my ears, trying not to think about what was happening next door. After awhile I'd warmed up slightly and stretched out my legs to distribute the warmth. Next my feet began to itch and with alarm, having suffered several minutes of this, I leapt out of bed and switched on the light. I went towards the bed, carefully took the edge of the sheet and pulled it back to reveal small red specks of blood all over its grimy surface.

I stood trembling, wondering what on earth to do.

The thought of re-entering Edwin's room, to find my rampant 'friend' in bed with him, was a horrific idea. At length, frozen to the bone, I decided I had no option but to knock hesitantly on the door. To my surprise he opened it fully dressed, as was Brenda, much to my relief. When he heard my news he said, "That's not good. I'd often thought that Mel was beast ridden as he never seemed to wash. Let me have a look." He gave the bed a rudimentary inspection. "Yes, you're right. I guess you're going to have to sleep with us," he grinned. I wasn't so happy.

We all hopped into his double bed, keeping on our underclothes, with him in the centre. He vacantly ran one hand up and down my body, as I lay rigid, hoping he wouldn't go any further. Soon I became aware that he was more interested in what lay on his other side. He rolled over, turning his back on me. I pressed into the wall in an effort to remove myself as far as possible from the heavy grunts and breathing noises coming from across the bed. An interminable time passed, then he mounted her, thrusting in and out for ages, until they both came gloriously and noisily together. I lay pressed against the wall, feeling sick with disgust and also envy, because my brief sessions of lovemaking had never been as ecstatic as theirs had sounded. The remainder of the night passed in an uneasy, half-sleeping, half-waking nightmare, as from time to time further grunting and heavy intercourse in various positions occurred. I lay helpless and hopeless, all confidence in my sexual ability and attractiveness to the opposite sex vanishing: a deadly and desolate feeling.

Dawn came at last. I crawled down to the bottom of the bed to avoid disturbing the lovers, with whom I'd no desire to communicate. I had a quick wash and hastily left. It was a crisp, cold morning, but I hardly noticed. I felt dead inside and unclean outside. I arrived at my mother's bungalow in time for breakfast and went round the back to admire the garden, which my stepfather kept in immaculate condition, rather like a public park. Red and yellow begonias and other colourful bedding plants bloomed prolifically in summer, but now there was little colour to soothe my spirits. My mum appeared at the kitchen window, then opened the door, a suspicious look on her face.

"Margaret! We didn't expect you until lunchtime. What have you been up to? You look like a tramp!" She was much shorter than me and stood, rubbing her hands nervously on her apron, her blue eyes holding little warmth. I muttered something about staying the night at a friend's and requested a bath.

"A bath! At this time of day! I'll have to put the immersion on." I thanked her and she grudgingly added, "Would you like a cup of tea?" I sat sipping the tea while she bustled around. There was no sign of my stepfather – 'Big Jim', his six foot plus towering over my tiny mum. We had loathed each other since their marriage two years earlier. The only thing he had in common with my father was his height. My dad had died when I was eleven and I'd got used to having Mum to myself.

I sank into the hot water, hoping to drown any foreign bodies clinging to my flesh, vigorously rubbing and scrubbing in the bubbles. Back in the kitchen I was greeted by a cold atmosphere, as my mum and step-dad regarded me with hostility in their eyes. They'd obviously been discussing me while I was in the bath, Jim, as usual, dreaming up the worst case scenario.

"Well, Margaret, your mother and I have been

wondering about you. Are you pregnant?" I was startled by this sudden accusation.

"Of course not! How could you think that?" He didn't look convinced.

"What were we to think? You come here demanding a hot bath, to get rid of the baby, we concluded." I found this almost laughable it was so ridiculous, but at the same time realised that if I were to get into that condition, I'd find no sympathy nor shelter at home.

Our breakfast was eaten in silence, my feeble attempts at conversation receiving no response. I went to my clean bed and slept until midday, then escaped to visit some girlfriends. Two of them were getting engaged, making me feel that I'd soon be left on the shelf – a daft thought for a seventeen-year-old. Back home at teatime I received a friendlier reception and chatted about my studies and other safe subjects. Afterwards I decided to return to Edwin's to check up on Brenda, who I assumed was still my friend. She seemed pleased to see me and was already tiring of his company. We went dancing on the pier, leaving him to go to the pub with his pals. At the dancing she became very moody; we had a big argument about her behaviour and I left, vowing to break off our friendship.

The remainder of the Christmas holidays passed peacefully. A truce had been declared at home and I managed to have some time alone with Mum, helping with the cooking and housework. I was looking forward to going back to Glasgow and keen to resume my studies. Mum came to the station and we had an emotional farewell as I boarded the London train. Crossing to Euston station I joyously jumped onto the Glasgow train. I loved every minute of the journey, gazing out the window as the landscape gradually became more interesting, the flatness disappearing and the hills beginning, until the sheep dotted moors and mountains of the borders came into view. As the train drew into Glasgow station, I could hardly hide the excitement I felt at being back again in that glorious city, wondering what surprises it held in store for the coming term.

Seven

On the first Friday evening I returned to the discotheque, hoping to see Duncan, but unsure of the reception I'd receive. I had made a devout New Year's resolution to give up sex and naively thought that we could have a chaste relationship. He was nowhere to be seen, but Adelina and Maria were there. "Hi Margaret, it's great to see you. How was your holiday?" Maria asked.

"It was really good, but I'm glad to be here – it feels like home now," I laughed, feeling it to be true.

"Guess who was here last week?" Adelina teased. I felt my heart rate increase, "Duncan! And he was asking after you, wondering when you'd be back," she smiled at my face, which was a mixture of consternation and happiness.

"Is that right? You know he finished with me before the holidays? Maybe he's changed his mind? I don't know how I feel about that," I admitted.

They commiserated with me, but had more exciting ideas in mind. "We're planning our summer holiday to Italy. We went last year and had a fantastic time, lazing on the beach all day and dancing and romancing every night. The Italian guys are so *hot,* not like the Brits," Maria enthused.

"It sounds wonderful," I said wistfully, imagining the hot sun and hotter boys.

"Why don't you come with us?" It was a tempting invitation and I had some savings, so I agreed. The following day we met and booked, which made me strengthen my resolution to avoid pregnancy.

That night this resolution was put to the test. After reserving our holiday we had gone for a drink, and had several rum and cokes to put us in a dancing mood. The disco seemed to have a warmer ambience, the music a stronger beat and the dancers greater rhythm. We burst in, giggling and joking, not noticing our respective boys, who were skulking in the corners watching us.

I felt a tap on my shoulder and looked round. Duncan stood, looking shy and lost. "Oh, Duncan, hi, it's great to see you," the rum spoke.

"It's guid tae see you too. I've missed you. I wish I hadnae said what ah said," he rubbed his hands together nervously, avoiding my eyes.

The alcohol filled me with delight, but a tiny part of my mind twinged with foreboding, which receded as he wrapped his arms around me to the strains of the Righteous Brothers, *'You've lost that lovin' feelin', now it's gone, gone, gone. . .'*

When the dancing was over he asked if I'd like to go for a drive. *Oh no, not that again. You know what'll happen.* My voice came out surprisingly strong, "No thanks, Duncan. I'm tired and want my bed." He walked me up the street and we stood locked in each other's arms for ages. *Maybe I should've gone for that drive? Remember your resolution, stupid.*

"Dae you fancy goin' for a drink at ma local next Friday?" he was like an expectant puppy, drooling in anticipation.

"Okay, usual time?" It came out before I could stop it. *Oh dear. Now I've done it.*

The week passed by in a frenzy of work at college, the evenings filled with studying, although my mind wandered constantly towards Friday as I sat in my tiny room pouring over my books.

He arrived punctually, as promised, and we spent an agreeable time drinking and chatting about nothing of any great importance, although at one point he became serious. "I cannae help wondering why you're still goin' oot wi' me? What dae ye see in me?" He seemed genuinely intrigued, but I could only shrug my shoulders and laugh in answer. *Yes, I've asked myself that question many times. I guess I love you, whatever that means.*

After this he steered the conversation into calmer waters. Neither of us were capable of articulating our feelings, taking big gulps of our drinks to ease the awkwardness. We left the pub and he suggested going for a drive. I agreed. *What a surprise! As if I didn't expect he'd suggest that. Well, I've got to either stick to my resolution or ask him about contraceptives.*

He turned off the engine. There was no time for talking. His tongue explored my right ear, his teeth nipped my earlobe, his breathing became faster and faster. *I've got to say something now. Stop, stop!* I was stifled by his kisses, as he pulled my knickers down round my ankles, his hot penis sliding into my aching, throbbing vagina, whose juices were running down my legs, so randy was I after such a long abstinence. He must have felt the same, for having completed the first session, after only a few minutes he was hard and raring to go once more. As he entered me for the second time my hot, whirling senses screamed, *you've done it this time for sure.* For an instant all caution left me as I completely relaxed, letting the whole of his sperm spurt up inside me, as we came together in one huge, trembling orgasm – the first that I had ever experienced. We lay silently entwined until he again made love to me for so long I thought my backside would smash right through the leather of the seat. This time I was past any feeling, being completely numb, but eventually he came and then collapsed across my breast falling instantly asleep.

I sat fondly stroking his hair. *How small and vulnerable he looks in sleep, like a little boy.* He would probably have slept all night like that, but my body became stiff and cold and I began to wriggle, waking him from his peaceful slumber. He kissed me blearily and began to pull on his clothes, whilst I did the same. We drove back listening in silence to the Beach Boys on the radio, *'Good, good, good, good vibrations . . .'*

He pulled up outside the hostel. "I'm off tae Edinburgh the morra wi' some mates. It's Scotland playing Wales in the rugby – should be a great game and a guid night in the pubs after, 'specially if we win," he smiled unconcernedly at me. *What? I thought we'd be together tomorrow night. How could he do that to me?* I had a lot to learn about men. "I'll see you next Friday, okay?" I nodded, trying to hide my disappointment.

We went to his local again the following Friday and indulged in another sexy session in the car in the woods afterwards but our lovemaking was not as rampant as the previous week. I was beginning to feel frustrated with the situation, with him only wanting to see me once a week. He gave me a goodnight kiss and announced, "I'm going oot for a pint wi' ma mates the morra night. It's Martin's birthday – we always celebrate it." *Lucky Martin. You should be with me you shit head.* I was extremely annoyed, but kept my thoughts to myself, simmering inside.

It continued like this for another three weeks and my feeling that he cared more about drinking with his pals than spending time with me increased. My hopes were raised when he took me to the pictures one Wednesday evening. It was a cowboy film, '*The Good, the Bad and the Ugly*', not my favourite, but it was certainly his, his rapt expression never faltering. It was good to be seeing him on a week night for a change and I expected to see him on Friday, but when we came out of the cinema he said that he was going drinking with his mates Friday and Saturday, but could see me on Sunday. My annoyance finally manifested. "Thanks Duncan for giving up your precious Sunday evening for me." With that I got out of the car, slamming the door.

Eight

As the weekend approached I decided that I was not going to sit around waiting for Sunday night and arranged to go to the Locarno ballroom with Adelina and Maria on Friday. It was a complete change from the disco – a huge hall filled with ghastly-looking boys, all far too young for us, who were lining the walls eyeing up the girls dancing together in the centre of the floor. It was exactly like a cattle market and we reluctantly joined in as we were dying for a dance. It wasn't long before we were besieged by dozens of the lads, who could at least dance.

This continued until near the end of the evening when suddenly a tall, slim young man with curly, chestnut-coloured hair and jade-green eyes asked me to dance. At once the whole room became transformed into a far more agreeable place. He was immediately likeable, his eyes smiling at me as we danced to the Four Tops hit of the moment, *'Reach out and I'll be there';* very apt I thought. My period had been due that weekend, but I was determined not to worry as the pills I'd taken the previous month had probably interfered with my sequence, I thought optimistically.

We continued to dance until the final 'smoochy' number, *'A Whiter Shade of Pale',* by Procol Harum. I swayed in his arms, feeling guilty but nevertheless thoroughly enjoying the sensation of being held close by him. When the music ended he offered, "Can ah see ya hame?" his Glaswegian accent even stronger than

Duncan's. I acquiesced and as we walked along I learnt that his name was Andy and that he worked in the ship building industry, which was on the verge of collapse. When we reached the hostel he didn't attempt to kiss me and asked, "Are ya daeing anything the morra evenin'?"

I was thrown into confusion: *oh, no! I really like him, but what about Duncan? What should I do? Well, Duncan shouldn't have gone away for the weekend – he obviously doesn't care too much about me. Just say 'yes'.*

"Look, if ya huv something else on, dinnae worry. We can meet up another night, mibbe?"

"No, it's all right. I'm not doing anything," I said without a twinge of guilt.

"Great, ah'll come here tae meet ya. Is eight o'clock okay?"

"Yes, fine. I'll see you then," I replied, feeling pleased to have something to do, and with such an attractive person. With that he was off, pausing to turn and wave as he strode up the road.

A short time before we were due to meet the next evening there was a knock on my door. Startled, as no-one ever came to my door, I opened it to find one of the hostel workers. "There's a phone call fur ya in the lobby," she informed me. I followed her wondering, *Who on earth can this be? Nobody phones me. It must be something urgent.* I'd given up hope of Duncan ever phoning. Most of the girls received calls from family and boyfriends, chatting on the line for ages, annoying others who were impatiently waiting. Phones in our rooms were a luxury the hostel could not afford and mobiles were yet to be invented.

I picked up the dangling receiver, "Hello? It's Margaret. Who's there?"

"It's Andy. Ah wis walking alang the street near yur place this afternoon, 'n thought ah passed ya, but ya ignored me."

He sounded frantic, but I soon placated him. "I wasn't even out this afternoon, so it couldn't have been me. You must've been hallucinating!"

"Och, that's a relief. Ah'll be there in aboot five minutes, okay?" I was ready, so I went outside and there he was, coming down the road looking smart in dark blue jeans and a green jumper which matched his eyes perfectly. "Margaret, ya look great! Sorry aboot that call – it must've been yur twin sister ah saw. Wid ya like tae gang for a bevvy?"

"Yes, that'd be great," I answered, happy to be out with such a charming, handsome young man. He took me to a pub not far from the hostel, which was full of folksy types from the art college. They were a fascinating-looking crowd: beautiful girls, with long, flowing hair and ankle-length, paisley-patterned skirts leant against long-haired boys with straggly beards, colourful jumpers, or tie-dye shirts worn over bell-bottomed, tatty jeans. Andy seemed to be a regular there, nodding to quite a few of them as he made his way to the bar.

"Let's gae 'n sit ower there, away frae this crowd," he suggested, and I followed him to a cosy, dimly-lit corner. "Cheers!" We clinked our glasses together – my Bacardi and coke and his pint of export, looking long into each other's eyes. We chatted away far more easily than had ever happened with Duncan and he appeared to be totally engrossed with me: a new and flattering experience.

When the pub shut he took me to a Folk Club, where we sang (or rather he sang and I listened) until the early hours of the morning. I loved folk music and enjoyed hearing him sing, far more melodically than Edwin. He escorted me home again and this time he kissed me goodnight. As his lips met mine I felt a tingle shoot through me, and was ashamed to think: *Oh, this feels so much better than Duncan's slobbery, wet kisses. Ah . . .these are exquisite. Oh, ah . . .!*

Eventually we disentangled ourselves and he asked, "Can ah see ya some time this week?"

Oh dear, I'm seeing Duncan tomorrow. I don't know what to do or how I feel. "Oh Andy, I'm really sorry, but I'll be busy studying all week. They give us loads of work." I needed time to sort out my thoughts about him and Duncan and the whole situation.

"Okay. How's aboot Friday? Ye'll be wanting a break frae yer books by then, surely?" He looked at me questioningly, smiling his lovely smile.

"Right. Friday should be fine." I wasn't too sure about this. I'd have to see what happened with Duncan first, but I grinned confidently at him.

"Guid. See ya here same time, okay?" I agreed and went to sleep exhausted by the turmoil in my head over these two boys – I wasn't used to this!

Nine

Duncan turned up as planned the following evening and we drove out to his local hotel once more. I was in a sombre mood which seemed to affect him, and we sat drinking our drinks quietly. It did not deter him from driving to our usual forest parking place, where he began to kiss me. I started to cry, remembering the other kisses; it just wasn't the same, and a huge coldness spread from inside me, engulfing me completely, numbing my senses. "What's wrong wi' you?" he kept asking, but I found it impossible to explain, my feelings of revulsion towards him being mixed up with the previous passionate ones of only the week before. *Why am I feeling like this? It was so wonderful and I might be pregnant by him. No! Don't think that. It can't be true.* "Can I see you next Friday?" he wanted to know, no doubt utterly bewildered by my behaviour.

"I'm sorry, Duncan, but I can't." He didn't say anything and we parted without being able to communicate our innermost feelings to each other. At nineteen and seventeen we didn't have enough experience of life to either understand or resolve the situation.

*

I went out with Andy for the next three weeks and saw him at least three evenings a week – indeed he would have seen me nearly every night if I hadn't been firm about my studies for the approaching exams. He took me out for meals, something Duncan had never done, and to see films which we both enjoyed watching. He was also a complete gentleman, going no further than kissing me, with which I was content. I was becoming increasingly worried about my condition, being three weeks late. I'd almost convinced myself that I was simply missing a month, but had moments of blind panic when yet another trip to the bathroom drew a blank. Finally I decided to return to the lady doctor.

Tremulously I entered the surgery which I'd so ardently hoped I'd never have to see again. After waiting for about half an hour, my name was called and I nervously opened her door. "Take a seat. What can I do for you?" She regarded me with no sign of recognition, so I told her about my previous visit. She looked me up in her files, found my particulars and glowered at me from behind her desk. "Why are you here bothering me again? Surely your boyfriend could be educated to use contraceptives?"

I looked at her helplessly. "I was too shy to mention it to him – it just never seemed to be the right time."

She looked flabbergasted. "Well, I don't know what to say. You are an extremely stupid girl," she was busily writing a prescription, which she handed to me. "This is for more of the pills I gave you before, but remember they only work if you are *not* pregnant."

Mumbling "Thank you," I grabbed the prescription and hurried from the room. *Surely she never told me that before? In fact she never explained anything about the pills.* Maybe I hadn't been listening. Nonetheless, I fervently hoped they'd have the same miraculous effect – my trusty 'magic' pills. Five days passed without result, but I kept hoping because on the packet it proclaimed that something could happen for up to ten days.

Meanwhile, during all this anguish, I was still seeing Andy who seemed to become keener each time we met. One Friday evening he took me to a friend's flat, where he said there was a party. He opened the door with a key and then confessed, "Ah'm sorry aboot this, but ma mate's let us huv the place fur a wee bit, so that we can be alane taegither. Ya dinnae mind, dae ya?" He was looking at me earnestly, unsure of my reaction. I was shocked and amused. *Some gentleman! It was simply the lack of somewhere to do it that was stopping him.* He lived at home and the hostel was extremely strict about male visitors who were only allowed in the downstairs lounge.

"That's okay. I don't mind, honestly," I managed to say.

He looked relieved and stated, "Dinnae worry, ah've got a packet o' condoms, so ye'll be safe." *How amazing, he actually cares about me!* I had thought all men were the same – irresponsible. It was a pleasant change to be cuddling up in a double bed, so different from the cramped back seat of the car acrobatics. To be able to stretch out and relax between the sheets, taking our time, without thoughts of strangers staring through the windows, or cold draughts circulating around our posteriors, was indeed a luxury. But despite all these material comforts I didn't enjoy this first encounter with him, although he was kind and considerate. It just wasn't satisfying and no doubt my mental state didn't help me relax. Afterwards though I was content lying curled up against him, surrounded by warmth, encircled by his arms.

We saw each other with increasing frequency after

that night, although it was back to 'goodnight' kisses on the street. One evening, sitting in the pub, he came up with an interesting suggestion. "Ya ken Easter's comin' soon 'n ah wondered if ye'd like tae gae camping on the Isle o' Arran? Huv ya ever bin there?"

"No, I haven't and I've never been camping." *Won't it be a bit cold? I was thinking. Easter's early this year. The weather could be dreadful.* I didn't want to voice these thoughts because he seemed to be very keen on the idea.

"Och, it's a beautiful place wi' high moontains 'n fab beaches. Ye'll love it! Lots o' Glaswegians gae there on bank holidays 'n hae a grand time."

"Well, okay, I've got nothing planned so I guess I could give it a try."

"Great! Ah've got all the gear so just bring warm clothes an' boots, in case it's a wee bit chilly at night." *A wee bit chilly – that's probably an understatement,* I thought morbidly.

*

Good Friday dawned, with large, grey clouds scudding across the sky accompanied by a strong and bitterly cold wind. We met at Central Station and boarded the train bound for Fairlie Pier, placing our rucksacks in the luggage rack. Andy also had an enormous cardboard box containing his 'kerry oot' : cans of export and lager, which he downed can after can, as I watched him, slowly sipping at one myself in an effort to keep him company. He seemed to be a changed person, laughing raucously with the other occupants of the carriage, all bound for the same destination and likewise accompanied by their cardboard 'kerry oot' boxes.

On arrival the train disgorged its contents of now rather merry Glaswegians, who all made their way haphazardly to the Brodick ferry. The boat was packed from top to bottom, the bar overflowing, beer swilling all over the place, as with one accord they drank pint after pint, their sole aim in life. I sat pressed against the wall regarding the scene with disgust and bewilderment, already regretting my decision to come. The vessel rolled horribly from side to side, but the other occupants were blissfully unaware of this as they clung onto their glasses in jovial abandonment.

Eventually the ghastly journey ended and we trudged out upon the Arran countryside, battling against freezing gusts of wind and rain. Andy turned to me and yelled, against the noise of the gale, "Ah'm meeting a pal o' mine in the pub. Ah gave him ma tent an' he's putting it up at the camp site, so it'll be all ready fur us." *Well, that's good planning,* I admitted as I followed him to the pub, glad of my boots and waterproof jacket.

We entered the pub which was full of more folk downing pints and nips of whisky. The air was filled with the stench of cigarette smoke, beer and whisky fumes and steaming damp clothes. Andy shouted in my ear, "There's Rob o'er there, lets gae ower." We pushed our way through the throng to where Rob sat, bleary-eyed, surrounded by full and empty pint glasses, the tent sitting squarely beside him. "Hi, Rob. How yer daeing, mate?"

Rob made an effort to focus on Andy. "Is that ya Andy? Great tae see ya. Ah'm a wee bit the worse fur wear. Sorry mate, ah couldnae get the tent up."

"Ah, dinnae worry. What'ur drinking?"

"Ah've plenty here, thanks. Away ya gae."

Off Andy went to the bar, to my consternation. Returning with more pints he saw my worried face. "Dinnae worry, Margaret. We can put the tent up later. It's no dark yet. There's still loads o' time."

Later and still later it became; the darkness set in, very dark darkness, unlike Glasgow where the city's lights filled the sky with a haze of light, even on the blackest night. Closing time came at last and I thankfully emerged into the fresh air, leaving behind the stench of stale beer and vomit from the toilets, my clothes stinking of cigarette smoke. It had stopped raining and I thought longingly of curling up with Andy in the tent, I was so exhausted by the day's events. Andy, however, was loathe to leave the pub, and with difficulty made his way along the road carrying the tent.

"The camp site's ower there," he announced, waving his arm in its general direction. On we stumbled over rough grass for what seemed miles. Then he stopped. "Right, we're here. Ya hold the torch, Margaret, while ah put up the tent." *What a weird camp site. There's no sign of any other tents, toilet blocks or anything,* I wondered, but kept silent, shining the weak beam of the torch onto Andy's uncoordinated attempts to unpack the tent. We then tried to erect it, but the wind was so strong, we both had to hang on to it with all our might to prevent it blowing away. Finally it was up, but blowing about so fearfully that we had to scrabble about looking for boulders to hold it down. It was a very old and decrepit tent, without any pegs.

At last we both crawled inside, worn out with our efforts. Andy put his arm round me – a welcome warmth. "Och, Margaret. Ah'm so sorry fur all this, whit must ya be thinking o' me?" There was no civilised answer to this, so instead we kissed and cuddled, until feeling the damp seeping into me from the ground, I rolled on top of him and slept fully clothed like that for the remainder of the night.

We were rudely awakened from our slumbers in the morning by a gruff voice outside. "Dae yous ken where yous are, yous in there? Ye're in the middle o' the golf course! Ye'll need tae get packed up n' away frae here the noo, or there'll be trouble." The voice was followed by a large policeman's head, glowering at us and our embarrassing position (I was still lying uppermost).

We hurriedly resumed seated positions and Andy said, "Officer, we're really sorry, but we thought this wis the camp site, it wis sae dark last night." *So, it's 'we' now is it?* I wasn't too happy to be included in the blame.

"Aye, aye. Ah've heard it all before, laddie. Yous Glaswegians gae me mair work oan bank holiday weekends than in the rest o' the year put taegither. Just get oot o' here an' tak' this thing doon."

Out we clambered into the wind and rain, the policeman impatiently watching us with obvious distaste as we struggled to take down the offending structure which was ruining the beautifully kept turf. Once packed up he seemed satisfied, directed us to the camp site and marched disdainfully off in the opposite direction, no doubt in search of more troublesome Glaswegians.

We heaved our heavy rucksacks onto our backs and trudged dejectedly through the pouring rain to the camp site, where once again we battled with the wind to re-erect the very damp tent. It flapped like a wild thing in all directions, desperately trying to fly away from us and our efforts to keep it in one place. Finally it stood penned down by rocks and we crawled in and collapsed onto the sleeping bags, where we ate a cold breakfast of cereal and rolls, having no cooker. A hot drink was what I craved more than anything else and I longed for the comfort of the hostel and my warm bed.

When we'd finished eating Andy had a suggestion to make: "Let's gae back tae the pub. It's opening time an' it'll be warmer 'n cosier than being in here." I readily agreed that it would be better than the tent, which seemed to be in constant danger of taking off leaving us exposed to the cruel elements. The thought of drinking, or even smelling liqueur, made my stomach churn and I couldn't fathom how Andy still wanted to go near the stuff after the vast quantities he'd consumed the previous night. *A café would be the place to go and get a hot drink, if there* was *one in this godforsaken place.* Andy was obviously keen to return to the pub and I didn't have the heart to suggest this.

The pub was packed with the same crowd of raucous, drunk Glaswegians. I sat and endured it until we were turfed out into the bitter weather at the end of lunchtime. By then my stomach was heaving uncontrollably and on reaching the tent, which was about two miles away, I could only manage half a tin of pears for my tea. Andy ate the rest and a couple of pies he'd bought at the pub. After our extravagant meal Andy had another bright idea: "Ah'm thinking we may as well return tae the pub. It's baltic in here." What could I say? It was indeed freezing, so back we plodded to the ever popular pub. On the way I emptied the pears out of my stomach on the roadside. Andy was most considerate. "Ya poor thing – ya must've caught a chill."

"Hmm, you're probably right," I agreed, although I

was thinking that it might be connected to my condition, which hadn't improved at all. *The 'magic' pills hadn't worked.*

We left the pub early as I'd been in the toilet most of the time, and spent a miserable night sleeping fitfully while the wind and rain battered against the tent. In the morning I peered out of the flap to a splendid scene of snow-covered mountains. No wonder we were perished.

I stayed most of the day in the tent feeling nauseous and dozing, whilst Andy walked to the village for provisions. He brought back some tasty food, but I couldn't eat a thing. Later in the afternoon we discovered a large puddle underneath the groundsheet. Andy groaned, "Och, we cannae sleep anither night in this. Let's pack up an' gae back tae the pub. Mibbe we can sneak intae ma mates' lodgings fur taenight." We attempted to do this at closing time, but it was impossible as the landlady was on constant lookout for any intruders into her establishment.

"There's nothing else fur it, we'll huv tae gae tae the dancin' fur shelter. Ah'm sae sorry, Margaret. Dae ya think ya can make it?" I muttered that I thought I could and mutely followed him, being too weak to argue. It was a long trek up the road, the wind howling through the trees, but at least it had stopped raining. Eventually, through the gloom a wooden shack came into view, strains of wild music and the pounding of dancing feet reverberating through the air.

"It sure soonds like they're haeing fun," my companion gaily remarked as he pushed open the door. The place was packed with other woebegone, washed out campers, either sitting about on the floor drinking their cans, or dancing deliriously in the centre of the room. The band, which consisted of a fiddler, an accordionist and a drummer, kept up a strong pace as the boys and girls whirled around the floor emitting crazed cries. I felt too ill to appreciate any of this and intermittently dashed outside to retch, there being little left in my stomach. Then I went back inside to lean exhaustedly against Andy, who seemed to be surviving the dreadful weekend extremely well.

At 4am we walked back to the ferry and waited three hours until its arrival in the cramped waiting room with other poor souls, all of whom were trying to keep warm and doze. Couples cuddled together on wooden benches, while single folk lay on the hard floor, their rucksacks for a pillow. At last the ferry arrived and we went on board accompanied by a much more subdued crowd from the outward trip, all bedraggled and ashen-faced. I blended in quite well. In fact I stayed in the toilet most of the time and also on the train back to Glasgow, longing constantly for the comfort of my bed.

I shakily alighted from the train and we parted on the platform. "Can we meet up on Wednesday?" he wanted to know. "I hope ye'll be feeling better by then. Ah'm sae sorry fur such an awfy weekend. It couldnae huv bin much worse."

I weakly said "goodbye" and wandered off thinking that he must've gone off me for good, I had been such dreadful company, my appearance a disaster.

Ten

Back at the hostel I crawled into bed and slept until teatime when I was awakened by the arrival of my sister, who had come to Glasgow on a work's course for a week. "Oh, Jean, it's so good to see you," I greeted her as she came in and sat down on the end of my bed. I was so pleased to see her that I nearly cried. She was my big sister – ten years older than me and could always be relied upon to give sound advice.

"Well, Margaret, whatever have you been up to, sleeping at this time of day?" She listened while I told her all about my weekend's camping catastrophe, although I omitted to tell her my concern about the possible cause of the sickness.

"What you need is something to line your stomach. I'll away down to the kitchen and see what I can find," she said soothingly. She returned carrying a glass of raw egg whisked into milk, which made me feel much improved physically, but not mentally. I was desperate to unburden my troubles, and plucking up courage I falteringly began to tell her what I suspected: about the pills, my relationship with Duncan and subsequently meeting Andy. "You should first of all return to the doctor for a pregnancy test," she advised. Pregnancy test kits and their easy availability were still in the future.

"Oh, I couldn't go back to that doctor! It would be too embarrassing," I said.

"Okay, well you can find another doctor."

"I suppose so," I reluctantly agreed, but actually I didn't want to know. I couldn't face up to the situation at all.

"And what about the father?" she relentlessly continued, "I guess it must be Duncan because of the three week gap and you already being late when you met Andy."

"Yes, I'm sure about that," I nodded vigorously.

"Can you work something out with him?" she wanted to know.

How can I do this? I've lost touch with him and I don't even know how I feel about him now. It's all such a mess. These thoughts went through my head, but all I could mutter was, "Hmm, maybe." I looked at her sorrowfully and she managed a bright smile.

"Anyway, don't worry. If you are pregnant you can stay with us when the time comes." This was an enormous relief to me as I'd had visions of being put out on the streets when my dreadful condition became evident. Jean lived with her husband, Ken, near Inverness; they had no children at that time.

She continued to get me organised. "The Easter holidays will soon be here and you're still coming to stay with us, aren't you?"

"Yes. I'm looking forward to it." I managed to cheer up a little.

"Good. Okay, if you can't find a doctor here you may visit ours while you're up."

I felt cornered. It was no good. I was going to have to find out sooner or later. "All right. That's what I'll do," I conceded.

*

On Wednesday I met Andy as arranged. "It's great tae see ya looking better," he remarked and gave me a hug and a kiss.

"Thanks. I feel loads better and my sister's been visiting which helped." There was no way I was going to tell him about my fears, although I could have deceived him as I was fairly certain he would have done the 'honourable thing' and married me.

"Margaret, ah hope ya still want tae see me after that awfy weekend, but ah ken yur moving doon tae the college campus near Ayr next term. Wid ya come up tae Glesga some weekends?"

Gosh! He really is still keen on me! "I'll try to get up to see you and I'll give you my 'phone number at the college." I scribbled it down and handed it to him. After a parting cuddle we bid each other 'goodbye' and I watched as he walked away, uncertain of my feelings for him. They had cooled considerably since the weekend away, and with the increasing realisation that I was carrying Duncan's child, although I still found this hard to believe. I automatically thought of it as a 'thing' inside of me, which would be immediately removed at birth and adopted by a couple capable of looking after it. I'd never had any contact with babies nor any desire to babysit or take them out in their prams, like some of my other girlfriends had been keen to do.

*

The Easter holidays arrived and with them the appointment at my sister's doctor. I supplied him with a urine sample and received the result a few days later.

"Well, Mrs Pither, the result was positive and your baby's due around the end of October." This was my first experience of being called 'Mrs' – it wasn't the 'done thing' to refer to an expectant mother as 'Miss'. I slunk speedily out of his room not wishing to ask any questions, or indeed to answer any uncomfortable ones from him.

I received this blow with a great deal of enforced optimism, working out that I'd only miss one month of the next academic year, zooming rapidly out of hospital and back to college as I planned to have the baby adopted. Various well meaning people informed me that the hospital staff were full of consideration for the unmarried mother who had decided to adopt, looking after the baby themselves if the mother said she didn't wish to see it. Obviously this would be the best way to do it, I concluded, because if I had only a peep at the infant I was certain that its little face would haunt me for the rest of my life.

My sister kept me busy sawing wood, cleaning windows and digging up her new garden ready for planting potatoes. This all helped to keep my mind off my troubles as well as giving me the faint hope that these strenuous exertions might dislodge the offending growth inside me. Alas, this was not to be the case. Many women seemed to lose their babies if they so much as sneezed too hard. Mostly they were happily married and longing for a family – it was most unfair. At seventeen, unmarried and at the beginning of my career I naturally didn't want to be saddled with a child, but I was so unbearably fit no amount of exertion had a detrimental effect on my pregnant state. Such is the twisted logic of life.

Eleven

At the end of the holidays I returned to college this time at the main site of Auchincruive, just outside Ayr, for the summer term. The campus was in a beautiful setting, with the river Ayr running through mature woodland surrounded by fertile farmland. The site had been a country estate and the fine mansion house was where we had lectures and dined on delicious home grown food. Students were accommodated in other buildings, the boys' and girls' dormitories separated by a long driveway. Sometimes the lads played tricks on us. One night they managed to get into our laundry room and seized our sexiest-looking lingerie. The following morning we were greeted by our bras and pants festooned across bushes, branches and fences, fluttering in the breeze, as we walked up the drive towards the main house. When we entered the breakfast room we were met by gales of laughter, our undies stuffed in our pockets. We had a lot of practical lessons and the fresh air combined with my condition gave me a healthy appetite. I bloomed but showed no outward signs of pregnancy, apart from the discomfort of budding breasts which gave me a certain satisfaction. I confided in no-one.

One weekend I went up to see Andy after one of his phone calls. It felt strange to be with him again. I realised that my feelings had changed so I finished our relationship, keeping my pregnancy a secret. I increasingly began to think about Duncan so I contacted him one evening on impulse. Luckily he answered the phone. "Och, hi Margaret, how's it going? Ah havnae seen you aroond." His voice betrayed little emotion.

"I'm down at the college near Ayr now for the summer term."

"Och, right. Will you be coming back up here?"

"No. Next year I'll be here." My course was for two years with only the first two terms spent at the Glasgow site.

"Och, I'll nae see much o' you then. Guid luck wi' yur studies," was his reply.

You need to tell him now! He's going to ring off soon. My heart was hammering, my mouth bone dry. I couldn't do it. "Okay, thanks. All the best." I put down the receiver in despair.

As the term continued I ate more and more, partly out of misery but mostly through sheer greed, the food was so fabulous and the helpings so huge. I began to feel heavier but just looked fatter all round, so nobody noticed anything abnormal about me. Then about a week before half term I started to feel sick with abdominal pains. One evening the pain became acute through my right side. I lay on my bed clutching my side. I could hardly breathe it was so bad. One of my room-mates, a kind African girl, noticed my plight. "Margaret, what's wrong?"

I managed to groan, "I don't know. I have an awful pain."

"Wait a minute," she said and returned with a cold flannel which she placed on my fevered brow, at the same time asking another girl to run to the matron.

The matron took one look at me. "I'm going to phone

the doctor," she stated. I began to panic. *Oh no! Now they'll discover about the baby!* I'd been visiting the local doctor regularly for antenatal check-ups on the quiet.

When he arrived I looked at him pleadingly through my gasps and groans. *Please keep my secret,* I silently prayed. "Don't worry, Margaret. I'm just going to examine you," he consoled soothingly and began to feel my abdomen carefully. After much prodding he announced, "I think you might have acute appendicitis. I'm going to phone an ambulance." Secretly I fantasised that I was having a miscarriage and the doctor had told them it was appendicitis to cover up my condition, which was no doubt ridiculous.

The ambulance arrived in no time and my roommates and the matron gathered at the entrance as they stretchered me out, "Get well soon! You'll be back in no time." They cheerily waved as I slid into the back of the vehicle which zoomed off, blue light flashing. It was all extremely exciting.

At the hospital I was given a thorough examination but no mention was made of my pregnant state, so I assumed that they'd not been informed about it, which I found rather puzzling. The doctor told me, "We're going to starve you overnight and decide in the morning whether or not to operate. Try to get some rest. We'll give you a sedative to help." Gratefully I snuggled down for the night, the pain already diminishing. I slept reasonably well and on waking the pain had lessened considerably. The doctor came and said, "That's good that the pain is less. We'll keep you in on a light diet and monitor your condition." He smiled at me reassuringly and I enjoyed cornflakes, a slice of toast and a cup of tea, joking with the other women in the ward. They kept me in for three days which I enjoyed, playing card games and chatting with the poor souls incarcerated there, who were all in a truly unhealthy condition, unlike myself. After three days the pain had subsided completely and I was released, complete with appendix and foetus, feeling much better and thinner. I decided that the pain must have originated from my massive food intake and consequently cut down to a more normal diet.

*

With the imminent approach of the half term holiday I realised that I had better tell someone at college my news. The obvious person was the female social worker and I entered her office nervously. "Come and sit down, Margaret. What can I do for you?" she manoeuvred her chair into a more congenial position away from her desk, her friendly face putting me more at ease.

I sat searching for the right words: then they came out in a rush. "I'm afraid I'm expecting a baby at the end of October, but I'm not going to keep it. It'll be adopted and I want to come back here straight after and finish the course. I'll study really hard to catch up with the work." I paused for breath, fiddling frenziedly with my fingers.

"Well, Margaret, that *is* news. You must be about four months already. I'd never have guessed! I think it might be possible for you to return in November, assuming there are no complications, but you'll have to see the Principal – he'll have the final say." This was a blow. The thought of telling the Principal filled me with fear. The kind social worker read my mind. "Don't worry, I'll inform him about your position to give him time to consider the situation before you meet him."

"Oh, thank you," I breathed with relief, nevertheless not relishing the prospect.

I didn't have long to wait; she arranged an appointment for the following afternoon at the end of my classes. The Principal, a tall, lean grey-haired man, whose warm brown eyes regarded me compassionately through large-lensed spectacles, ushered me to a padded chair near him. "It's good to see you, Margaret. I don't know what it is about our horticultural students – you know one of the girls last year was also in this predicament?" This was news to me and I wondered what had happened to her. I was soon to find out. "Like you she was due around October and would have missed at least a month's work. This is, quite frankly, too much to make up. The work load in the second year of the certificate course is considerable and you'd be struggling to keep up."

I was becoming more and more agitated and interrupted, "But I'd study and work really hard. Please let me come back," I pleaded desperately, not knowing what else I could do for that year to distract my mind from what had happened.

"I'm afraid it's just not possible, Margaret, but you may return the following year, that is if you don't decide to keep the baby." He looked at me with pity and concern, reactions that I would increasingly experience as the time for my confinement drew nearer.

"Of course I won't keep the baby! How could I bring it up on my own? It would be impossible, and anyway I don't want to," I cried emphatically.

He spoke calmly and sympathetically, "You're very young and in a vulnerable position. You may be more upset by the birth than you realise and in all probability you'll decide to keep your child. That's what happened to last year's student. Have you got any family who'll support you?" I muttered that my sister had offered to take me in for the period before the birth, but was not expecting me to keep the baby. "Well, that's something, isn't it? I wish I could be of more help, but in this situation you'll just have to wait and see how you feel after the birth, won't you?"

"Yes, I suppose so," I unwillingly agreed, sensing deep down that he might be right but not wishing to face up to that unthinkable possibility.

Twelve

I went home for the week's holiday determined to keep my condition a secret, but when I saw my mum my feelings altered. For the first time since childhood a great love and need of her swept over me. I cried myself to sleep; I didn't want to leave and craved her compassion and forgiveness. As for 'Big Jim', I knew that he'd never entertain the prospect of looking after me. He regarded unmarried motherhood and its immoral cause as an almost unimaginable, unacceptable and unforgivable position, despite the fact that he'd had to marry his wife as a result of similar behaviour.

At dinner one day my stepfather commented, "Margaret, you seem to have put on a lot of weight. It must be all that delicious college food, I suppose?" One look at his suspicious face and I knew that lying would be useless. I couldn't meet his eyes and broke down, sobbing uncontrollably. "You're pregnant, aren't you." It was a statement, not a question and my sobs grew louder and louder.

I longed to be alone with Mum, crying in her arms, feeling her love and sympathy engulfing me. But this wasn't going to happen. Even as a small child when I crawled upon her knees craving cuddles, she would push me off, saying, "Oh Margaret, you're too heavy" and I'd be unceremoniously dumped on the floor, a hollow hole in the depths of my being.

All Mum supplied me with was a box of tissues. I sat

sniffing and snuffling while they waited to begin the interrogation. Naturally Jim began it. "So, who's the father?"

I wiped my eyes again and blew my nose. "A boy I met at the disco. His name's Duncan."

"Hmm. And how old is he?" He glared sternly at me: it was like being in the dock.

"Nineteen. He has a good job in telecommunications and lives with his parents in a posh part of Glasgow. He's an only child." I hoped this information would mollify him somewhat.

"Well, he should be able to provide for you and the child. When's it due by the way?" There was no end to his questioning. Mum sat staring out of the window to the garden, her favourite place, no doubt trying to gain some solace from the plants.

"My date's the end of October. I haven't told Duncan and we've stopped seeing each other. It's not easy now I'm at Auchincruive." My lame excuse hung in the air.

My stepfather guffawed grimly, "Oh my god! You'll need to tell him, won't you, you foolish girl. He'll have to do the right thing by you and marry you, as soon as possible. You certainly can't stay here with us," he proclaimed, no doubt remembering when he was in a similar position, but dismissing the strong possibility that we'd be condemned to a miserable existence together for the rest of our lives.

No, I don't want this! Anger was now becoming uppermost in my head, which throbbed with its heat. "I don't need to tell him. I'm going to get the baby adopted and go back to college the next year."

Mum suddenly came to life, "But Margaret, once you

have the baby you won't be able to part with it. Your hormones change with the birth and you won't be able to resist the motherly instinct," she said, almost kindly.

This advice is totally useless! They won't care for me or their grandchild, so what's the point? I fumed, "They'll take it away as soon as it's born – I won't have to see it or look after it, so it'll be easy," I exploded, my face burning, my heart thumping.

This was too much for Mum. She fled to her bedroom, clutching her hanky, where the sound of her sobs could not be stifled. Jim stood up, glaring at me with hatred. "Now look what you've done to your mother. Every time you come here you cause problems. I think you should pack your bags and leave in the morning," he ordered coldly. With that he went into their bedroom, no doubt to console her and shut the door. *I hate him! If Mum weren't married to him I'm sure it'd be different. She'd not tell me to leave. She'd love me and her grandchild cos she's my mum.* I was no longer angry. I went to my room, flung myself on my bed and howled and howled into my pillow, until finally I fell asleep, worn out with all the emotion, which doubtless Mum was also doing in her bed – but she had her husband to love and cherish her. I had nobody.

In the morning the atmosphere was tense, but calm. There was no sign of 'Big Jim' to my relief, but it was impossible to talk to Mum at breakfast because I didn't know what to say. I didn't want to upset her again and found it hard to stop myself from crying, so we ate in silence, the toast and cereal tasting like sawdust as I tried to swallow them. At last I was ready and waved goodbye to her from the top of our steps, trying not to show any emotion. The sadness inside was like a rock now: I needed to be strong to face a world which soon would know that I was a sinner, an unmarried pregnant girl, for that was how things were in the 1960s.

Thirteen

Back in Glasgow I booked into the hostel for a couple of nights and got allocated my old room. I sat on my bed feeling bereft, the absence of my mother overwhelming me with sadness. There was only one other person I craved to see – Duncan. I trudged downstairs to the phone and dialled his number. A man's voice answered. "Hello, is that you Duncan?"

"Nae, this is his father. And you are?"

My pulse quickened: I hadn't expected to be confronted by his dad. Did they even know of my existence? Probably not. "Oh, it's just a friend," I said hesitantly.

"And does this friend hae a name?" He didn't sound too pleased.

"Yes, it's Margaret," I reluctantly admitted.

"Okay, ah'll call him," he offered unwillingly.

I stood trembling in the hallway, unsure of what to say. "Hi Margaret. Long time no see – how ya daeing? Are you still at Auchincruive?" His voice sounded as gorgeous as ever and I longed to see him.

"Yes, but I'm in Glasgow for the next two nights, back at the hostel. I've just been home for a holiday."

"Och, yous students, yur always on holiday, no like us hard-working folk," he quipped.

I felt encouraged by his banter and asked, "Do you

fancy meeting up tonight?" It was early on a Saturday evening.

"Och, nae. Sorry. I'm away oot drinking wi' ma mates taenight," he said with relish.

You've got to tell him now! It's your last chance, I ordered myself, feeling sick and scared. I took a deep breath and spoke into the mouthpiece, my hand trembling, "That's too bad. I really wanted to see you tonight to tell you something." It was still hard to put into words.

"Well, you'd better tell me noo, whatever it is," he replied.

Finally it came out in a rush, "I'm pregnant with your child. It's due later in October." *So, that's it out. Please say you want to see me. Don't leave me!*

It took a few seconds for him to reply, "That's too bad, Margaret. I'll come 'n see you the morra afternoon. Will two o'clock be okay?"

I felt my tension dissipating – *he did want to meet me!*

"Yes, that's fine. See you then." I was keen to terminate our conversation before he changed his mind.

*

I spent the next morning in a state of anguish, wondering whether or not he would turn up; how I would feel if he did and what he would have to say, for surely now something definite would be accomplished. Just before two I hovered at the window, watching for his car. It appeared in the distance, but then went right past without stopping – with him, without a glance, at the wheel. I ran outside, thinking he'd return, but he never did. In shock I went to my room. *Why did he turn up and then not even stop?* It was a mystery. But then there was a knock on my door. It was the warden. "There's a phone call fur ya," she said.

I hurried after her, with dread. "Hello," I breathed helplessly, knowing it would be him.

"I'm phoning tae tell you tae have nae illusions aboot me," his voice sounded cold and cruel, shattering my hopes and dreams. He continued remorselessly, "Ah dinnae believe the wean's mine."

I interrupted, pleading, "It is! The dates fit with when I was seeing you."

"But why did you finish wi' me? I bet you were seein' some other guy," he yelled angrily.

I was forced to admit it. "Yes, I was. But we didn't do anything for a while, so it must be yours," I said weakly.

"So, I was right. And are you still seein' him?"

"No, I'm not. I finished with him cos I only want to be with you," I blabbed.

"I dinnae believe you. I want nothing mair tae do wi' you, do you hear me?" he shouted, slamming down the receiver.

I shakily went back to my room, feeling totally deserted and wanting my mum more than ever. The room where I had suffered all the past agonies of love, passion, worry and misgiving. I threw myself on the bed sobbing in utter desolation, until I fell asleep exhausted.

In the morning I returned to college and the remainder of the summer term passed quickly, with little time to reflect on my condition. The place was so beautiful that it calmed my turbulent thoughts – the fruit and vegetables ripened in the sunshine in conjunction with the ripening taking place inside of me. I only became troubled in bed at night when they rose to the surface, until submerged by blissful sleep.

*

At the end of term I went to stay with my sister, who was a great source of strength. She had no children of her own and was not filled with concern about my impending motherhood. We were equally casual about my pregnancy. I was still firmly fixed upon adoption and rarely became weepy and motherly as I was certain that my life would be ruined if I decided to bring up an infant single-handed. My head was filled with wild schemes of working abroad in the period between the birth and my return to college the following year. Distant shores beckoned enticingly, arousing my dormant desires to explore the world. I'd had to cancel the Italian holiday with Maria and Adelina, who had been full of sympathy when they'd heard my news.

In order to pay for my keep I obtained a shop assistant position with Boots the Chemist in Inverness. I was amazed when they offered me the job, convinced that they would have noticed my condition at the interview: I was six months pregnant!

Each morning at eight thirty I dashed into the cloakroom. I hastily removed my copious duffel coat, my back turned towards the rest of the staff, and slipped into the regulation blue overall, which fortunately was loose-fitting. I struggled through the day until six o'clock, standing all the time, except for two fifteen minute tea breaks and an hour's lunch. Luckily my bladder was young and strong and little affected by the baby. One of the other assistants was four months pregnant – she was allowed to sit down when the shop wasn't busy. I had to just grin and bear it, my poor feet swollen and aching; I was learning fast that being an unmarried pregnant woman was no joke, but fortunately my condition was scarcely noticeable because of my height.

During this period a maiden aunt came to visit us: there was no question of divulging my secret – we simply prayed that she wouldn't notice. I was busy knitting a strange garment – not for the baby, but for myself. It was a dress, with horizontal stripes of glittery white, red, black and turquoise wool, all the rage at that time. Soon after our Aunt Pat arrived, she remarked at the breakfast table, "Margaret, I hope you don't mind me saying, but you appear to have put on rather a lot of weight." She looked at me with concern on her freckled face.

"Oh, I guess it's all the yummy college food. Don't worry, I'll lose it all soon." *If only you knew how soon!*

"Well, let's hope that's the case, but in the meantime maybe you should consider drinking less milk at breakfast?" Her eyes rested on the full glass in my hand.

I shifted nervously in my seat, praying that she wouldn't guess the real need for the extra milk, while Jean sat opposite, not meeting my eyes and trying not to laugh. "Hmm. You're probably right – I'll cut down soon," I muttered, taking another gulp.

Aunt Pat was unimpressed. "And another thing. That garment your knitting is rather inappropriate."

I was flabbergasted! *This is going too far, but I must stay calm.* "What do you mean, inappropriate?"

She continued, undaunted, "Surely you must realise that horizontal stripes make you look bigger? They can only be worn by thin people," she explained.

I decided not to even bother replying to this and left the table, barely suppressing my irritation. Jean told me later that our aunt had hoped that she hadn't offended me, she was only expressing her concern. After she'd left my sister and I laughed about it and wondered if she really had thought it was fat. Later, when she learned the truth, she assured us that she'd never dreamed of anything so shocking.

After a month I was forced to leave Boots – my legs and feet could no longer stand the strain, and my belly was becoming increasingly difficult to hide under the overall. It was time to put my feet up.

Fourteen

I had to attend antenatal clinics at Inverness Hospital, where I was to give birth. These ordeals were a nightmare. I sat waiting on the hard chairs, gazing vacantly at the posters on the walls, all of which were aimed at expecting mums and their soon to be cherished offspring – *I didn't want to know.* Surrounding me were the enormous shapes of maternal, married mothers-to-be, pervading the atmosphere with their pungent, pregnant odour. This, mixed with disinfectant fumes, made me feel nauseous and I longed to be outside inhaling the fresh air. I remained as aloof as I could accomplish in a situation designed for maximum loss of dignity.

My name was called, "Mrs Pither, this way please," the short, stout nurse began leading me down a long corridor.

Affronted, I engaged her attention, " By the way, I'm a 'Miss', not a 'Mrs', and I'm not likely to become one in the near future," I loftily informed her.

She stopped, regarding me unsympathetically. "It's the hospital's policy to refer to all pregnant women attending the clinics as 'Mrs'; this avoids any embarrassment." *That's me told – I'll just have to accept being 'Mrs' from now on,* I reluctantly admitted, as I was herded from room to room. This seemingly endless checking of my condition I found boring and time consuming; I felt completely separate from the bulge which was the subject of so much attention and whose existence I was hardly able to comprehend.

*

The final two months of my pregnancy passed slowly in utter seclusion at my sister's home, apart from the weekly clinic visits. At the weekends we went wild raspberry or blackberry picking, my balloon-like bump pushing aside the prickly stems, enabling me to grasp the biggest, juiciest berries, which no longer hung tantalisingly just out of reach. During the week my sister and her husband were at work all day. All morning I slept, my agonising thoughts receding into the abyss of slumber. In the afternoon I cooked their dinner and did the housework, gladly welcoming them home in the early evening, happy to have company. I placed my carefully prepared meal proudly on the table, but often was overcome by misery, rushing to my room leaving the food untouched, to sob for hours, until Jean knocked on my door. "Margaret, I've warmed up your tea. Are you ready to eat it now?"

The appetising smell wafted into my room, arousing my hunger. "Yes, okay. I'll come out now." Then I would eat while my considerate sister offered a few consoling words which usually cheered me up. Afterwards I'd fall asleep again, worn out by all my misery.

When I attended the clinic just two weeks before delivery 'D' day I was ushered into a larger room. A doctor entered and asked me, "Mrs Pither, a group of medical students are here today. Would you mind them examining you?"

Stop calling me Mrs Pither! I silently shrieked, calmly replying, "Of course, that's fine," a beatific smile upon my face.

"That's good. Please lie down on the bed and pull up your top." I did as I was told, peering at the room over my bump. He went to the door, "Right, you may come in now."

A group of around ten students, boys and girls not much older than me, filed into the room and stood awkwardly round my bed. "Okay, you may begin to examine the patient now," the doctor instructed. They took it in turns to prod painfully with their cold fingers – *why hadn't they warmed their hands first?* The prodding was accompanied by a great deal of muttering as I strained to make sense of their unintelligible chatter.

At length one of the learned young gentlemen smiled gleefully at me; by then I was lying staring blankly at the ceiling, removed from all that was happening beneath my non-existent waistline. He paused, swept the group with his eyes, and proudly announced, "Well, Mrs Pither, I think it might be twins. Wouldn't that be lovely?" The rest of the company showed their delight, all beaming at the happy mum.

Except that she wasn't. I produced my best grimace, "Actually, *doctor*, that would only double the trouble – I'm not married and have no intention of keeping the baby, or *babies,* thank you very much." The students laughed nervously, the girls gazing sympathetically at me, while the young men sheepishly tried to disappear into their white coats, the one who'd made the announcement almost vanishing from view. Then they all rapidly left the room as if the patient had suddenly contracted a highly infectious disease.

*

'D' day arrived and departed without a sign of baby or babies. This didn't disturb me in the slightest: I'd been doing my own calculations and was convinced that it would occur one week later. Five more days passed with no indication that the 'thing' in my womb wished to be removed from its warm and watery abode. The weekend arrived and as I sat watching the late night film, *Birdman of Alcatraz,* I beat rhythmically upon the bulge, hoping to galvanise it into action. Burt Lancaster's internment resonated with mine. I was in my own prison, gaining comfort from watching the comings and goings of the birds to my sister's bird table outside the kitchen window. All I craved was to be rid of the huge growth inside me, to escape from my own prison, to begin living again, to go dancing and all the other things an eighteen-year-old should be doing. Instead I was just a monstrous lump of flesh aimlessly lying around day after day.

At nine in the morning I was rudely wakened from my slumbers. I needed the toilet – fast. *What's this – diarrhoea?* Volumes of watery brown liquid poured out of me, but from the wrong place. I shouted to my sister, "Jean, Jean! Help! Something awful's happening." Finally rousing herself from her accustomed Sunday morning lie in, she came to the door. I was still stranded on the loo.

"Margaret, what on earth's the matter?" I explained what was happening. Neither of us had much idea about the birth process. I'd never had the courage to attend antenatal classes and had only heard vague old wives' tales, mostly from my mum. One of these concerned the 'bursting of the waters', (whatever that was) – if these burst first it was extremely dangerous; the baby would be left dry and damaged and death could result for mother and child. We both panicked, and Jean, still half asleep, ran down the road to phone an ambulance, without considering that her car was appropriate for such an emergency.

The ambulance duly arrived and I was bundled into it with my few belongings. My sister no doubt returned to bed with a sigh of relief, glad to be rid of me for a few days, after which I'd hopefully be back to 'normal'. I sat in the ambulance pondering about the previous night's prodding, which had possibly had an effect on the 'thing'. I was surprised that I felt no lighter after the huge liquid loss and imagined the baby bumping and bruising itself without its protecting fluid, desperate to escape from its host into an even more inhospitable outside world.

On arrival at the hospital a nurse escorted me to a room and ordered, "Mrs Pither, you must empty your bowels now."

"Oh, I already have," I informed her, but she still insisted that I sit on the toilet, where I was left for an age until eventually she gave up and told me to lie on the bed and wait. I waited and waited for hours feeling extremely bored with nothing to do.

There was no pain and occasionally a nurse would poke her head round the door and enquire, "Are there any developments?" On receiving a negative response, she'd quickly disappear. After a while I began to experience small twinges of what might be described as pain. *Ah, something's happening now – I must push down hard every time I feel one,* I thought, remembering tales of other women's labours, so dutifully I pushed as hard as I could with every twinge.

After about an hour of this, with no result from all my

hard work, a nurse peered through the door's glass and observed me scarlet-faced, pushing with all my might. She hurried in, glared at me and shrieked, "What do you think you're doing Mrs Pither?"

Calmly I explained, "I've been feeling pains so I'm pushing, cos that's what you're supposed to do." *How stupid is this nurse?*

She observed me with a mixture of amazement and despair. "You're in the second stage of labour, Mrs Pither, and should be resting and conserving your strength for the third and final stage. Then you may push away to your heart's content." After she'd gone I lay musing, mystified about these three stages. I'd been led to believe that it was all pushing and pain from start to finish.

My ruminations were rudely interrupted by the arrival of two nurses, one obviously in a senior position, who ordered, "Come on Mrs Pither, it's time to go to the delivery room." She helped me off the bed, attempting a smile. *Oh no, not the delivery room! This is too horrible,* I moaned to myself as they accompanied me along a long corridor to the place of torture. I could hardly walk for the urge to move my bowels, but they waved aside my lamentations, taking an arm each and dragging me along, the senior one saying, "It's only the baby, come on you must hurry."

Finally we reached the 'chamber of horrors' where I was forced to climb up on a bed so high it was a mountaineering feat to reach its dizzy summit. It was exceedingly hard and uncomfortable and my legs were placed in straps, forcing them wide apart, much to my embarrassment. But there was little time to experience this as a doctor ordered me, "Start pushing!"

There seemed to be dozens of nurses surrounding the bed, all shouting the same instruction, "Push, push!" But they were disappointed. I had no urge to comply with their wishes and felt more like sleeping.

The doctor admonished me, "You must push hard, Mrs Pither!"

The chorus of nurses shouted, "Push! Push!" Spurred on by all their shouting I managed a few faint muscular tremors, and after what seemed ages the 'thing' slithered out, was removed to the other side of the room, hung up by its long, skinny feet and its bottom smacked hard, whereupon it began to cry, which didn't really surprise me, the welcome it had received in this new world. It was the fifth of November but I didn't feel like letting off any fireworks.

The doctor announced, "It's a boy!" but I wasn't too curious, simply glad that it was over and I was rid of the bulge at last. I was wheeled out of the room along many corridors to a small ward with four beds, which were inhabited by two pregnant women and one new mum. It was 4.30pm, a mere seven-and-a-half hours since my sudden Sunday awakening. Jean phoned the hospital and was astonished to be informed of my speedy delivery. At visiting time she arrived with a box of chocolates to cheer me up. She listened patiently as I regaled her with all the gruesome details of the afternoon's events.

She sat looking at me with amusement, pleased at my perky state, and enquired hesitantly, "Would you mind if I had a wee peek at the baby? I'd really like to see what he looks like."

I wasn't too happy about this request, but reluctantly agreed. A nurse came to escort her to the baby room, where all the new born were kept. She returned, chuckling, pulled up a chair and asked, "Did you go with a Chinese man, Margaret?"

"What on earth do you mean, a Chinese man?" I cried in amazement.

She managed to stop giggling and continued, "Well, he looks Chinese with slit eyes, but I could tell he was yours by his feet."

I was becoming increasingly agitated. " What about his feet?"

"Well, they're enormous and flat-looking with long, skinny toes," she rejoined, "just like yours!"

"Thanks very much, dear sister," I quipped, but I was seething inside. *Surely I haven't given birth to such an ugly child?* Then I remembered Duncan. *Well, it might be possible . . .*

Although she had aroused my curiosity, I was determined not to surrender to my emotions. *I must not see him.* I knew that if I even glimpsed him for an instant it would be much more difficult to give him up; I was certain that adoption would provide him with a better life. He would be raised by loving parents in a good home with plenty of provision for his welfare. What did I have to offer him? A life lacking in wealth, comfort and security. *But what about maternal love?* Yes, maybe this – but was it enough?

Visiting time ended and Jean left, promising to return the next evening. I asked the nurses if it were possible not to see my son and they assured me that they'd be happy to look after him. All the other babies were cared for by their mothers after the first night, unless they were incapacitated in some way, and the nurses welcomed the opportunity for some infant care.

Fifteen

After breakfast the next day I was feeling strong and full of determination to go through with the adoption. Then the ward doors were flung open. In sailed Matron, a bevy of nurses trailing in her wake. She was the Supreme Being – her word was to be obeyed. *Without question.* She came to a halt beside my bed where I lay reading a romantic novel, thoughtfully provided by my sister.

She fixed me with her steely stare. My book tumbled to the floor. Her face was set in stone, her starched white hat pinned tightly to her grey bun, her bosom heaving under her white apron and blue uniform. I watched her mouth open wide as her words shot out, "You have to look after your child, girl. My nurses are *much* too busy." Shocked, I stared at her glaring, austere countenance and hopelessly realised my fate. No doubt she regarded me as a sinful woman who should be forced to pay for her sins. She glanced at her watch, positioned above her left breast, then strode purposefully out, the nurses following dutifully behind.

I lay in bed feeling a great dread descend upon me. In those days the minimum stay in hospital after birth was one week – a whole week of looking after my son, followed by leaving the hospital without him, never to see him again. *How can I do this?*

A while later he was wheeled in, fast asleep in his little cot. I lay in bed, my back turned towards him;

somehow I thought that by ignoring his presence he might magically go away again. Feeding time arrived and he awoke as if on cue, crying quietly while gazing at me with his slit-like eyes, which seemed full of reproach for having brought him into this world so thoughtlessly.

My sense of guilt grew and grew as I lay listening to his howls, trying to steel myself to pick him up. A nurse appeared and came over to his cot. "So you're the one making all this noise," she cooed, looking over at me with kindness in her eyes. Realising my dilemma she picked him up and gave him his bottle. "This is how you hold him," she instructed, continuing "and it's important to support his wee head as his neck's too weak at first to do it himself." She smiled down at my son with affection as he strongly sucked on the teat, his eyes staring fixedly at her face.

I sat watching this domestic scene with reluctant fascination, my eyes drawn constantly to his strange, small face, marvelling at his total concentration. "Thanks so much for feeding him," I said, adding, "I'm afraid I hardly know one end of a baby from the other. You see I've never had any dealings with them cos there's none in my family." I felt out of my depth and looked helplessly at her.

"Don't worry – you'll soon get the hang of it. It's time to get to know the other end of him now," she smirked, assembling all the paraphernalia needed for nappy changing. I watched, horrified at the nappy's tiny contents and the monstrous size of his genitalia in comparison with his tiny body. The nurse observed my gaping expression. "It's okay. All baby boys are like this; he's really not a monster!" I laughed nervously, becoming even more nervous as she removed a huge nappy pin from between her clenched teeth and plunged it into his towelling nappy, just above his vulnerable-looking belly button, so recently severed.

As the days went by I couldn't always rely on a passing nurse to take pity on me, and by the end of the week I was bathing, feeding and nappy changing with ease. I grew to enjoy these simple activities, especially the bathing, holding him in the warm, soapy water, watching his little body moving in pleasure, reminding him doubtlessly of his recent watery domain. Whenever I wasn't looking after him I tried not to dwell on our impending parting, still trying to convince myself that he'd be better off without me. As these thoughts were too painful to be thought for most of my hospital stay I was in a state of trance, removed from the whole painful situation.

The other women in my ward were fairly friendly towards me, especially the youngest, who dragged me from ward to ward each day. "Look at us!" she exclaimed, pointing to our still large and sagging abdomens. "We need to exercise big time to get rid of these – and remember to do your pelvic floor exercises, at least a hundred each day, to get in shape for *you know what!*"

One evening during visiting hours my sister arrived as usual. She was my sole visitor each night: her husband was too embarrassed by the situation to make an appearance. As we sat happily chatting to each other we gradually became aware of a commotion over the other side of the room. The husband of the oldest mum was weeping copiously into a large, white handkerchief. We stopped talking, wondering what could be the matter.

The man kept glancing over at us with a great many

sniffs and snuffles and we caught snatches of his wife saying, in hushed tones, "She's not married – how terrible – she has to give him up – foster parents – adoption – so sad – *how can she do it?*" We tried hard not to break out into hysterical giggles and when they spotted us listening the new father closed the curtains, giving us a last, tearful stare.

When I didn't have Jean to distract me at visiting times, I watched silently as each baby was lovingly visited by its father, each wife by her devoted husband, an overwhelming sadness enveloping me. *Still, it could be far worse,* I reasoned, *all others had deserted me, but at least I had my loyal sister.*

*

Finally the day dawned when I was to leave hospital and my small son. As I fed and bathed him for the last time, I felt such pain and desolation it was all I could do not to break down weeping when Jean came to collect me. Somehow I managed to control myself and we sadly left on a cold, wet November day. A few days later my baby also left the hospital to spend the following six weeks with foster parents in Inverness, while adoptive parents were being chosen for him. There was a long waiting list of childless couples anxiously hoping to adopt a fine, healthy baby boy just like him. I also had these six weeks to change my mind. I lived through the days as before, busying myself with housework and preparing meals, the pain a distant hum. But the nights passed in agony as I lay in bed imagining him breathing close beside me in his cot; I would see his little face gazing at me in the darkness, his eyes seeming to plead, *don't abandon me, I belong to you.* I fantasised that he would prefer to have a poor existence, with only his mum to care for him, instead of a cosy, easy upbringing with two parents.

During this period I regularly met with the Children's Officer who was arranging the adoption. I frequently burst into tears at these meetings, finding it harder and harder to accept the fact that my son would soon belong to someone else. The officer also informed me of his progress, which did little to console me, only increasing the urge to see him, as I heard about his rapid growth and good health. Although she was sympathetic to my distress, she counselled, "Margaret, adoption is the best option, both for you and your son, especially as he's a boy – it's even harder to bring up a boy on your own than a girl." *Why is that?* my mind cried.

Sixteen

As Christmas approached my despair and misery became increasingly intolerable with each passing day. The new clothes which I was going to buy with my savings to cheer myself up weren't bought. In the back of my mind an idea was growing – *maybe I can find a way to keep him?* Every penny would then be needed to look after him.

I went to see the Children's Officer and told her, "I've changed my mind – I'd like to keep my son."

She did her best to discourage me. "Have you really thought this through, Margaret? It's a huge responsibility for you to raise him on your own." She regarded me with sympathy, but there was a hint of irritation in her voice.

I shifted nervously in my seat. *Of course I haven't thought it through, I just know I want to keep him.* "Well, my sister may be able to help, at least at first," I hesitantly suggested, not being sure of Jean's reaction.

"Okay, I'll arrange a meeting with her," was the reply.

*

A few days later she discussed it with Jean. "Of course they can stay with us until Margaret finds somewhere else to stay, it's not a problem," she said confidently, brushing aside thoughts of commotion and chaos coming to her calm home.

"Well, that sounds like a positive step. I'll contact the Social Work Department in Edinburgh: they might be able to find her a housekeeping post. That's the only way she's going to be able to obtain accommodation and employment easily, at least in the short term," she said.

Jean came home that night and told me what had happened. Then she added, "You know, Margaret, I've been desperately wanting to become a doting aunt, but I didn't like to say as your mind seemed to be set on adoption." We both hugged each other, laughing deliriously, until her husband, Ken, came in demanding what all the fuss was about. He accepted the decision, secretly looking forward to his new role as uncle.

The plan to be a housekeeper did not appeal to me, although I did want to settle in Edinburgh. Glasgow held too many memories and Inverness was too northerly for my taste, but Edinburgh was Scotland's vibrant capital offering wider career prospects. I made a decision: I would seek a housekeeping position and then start looking for a proper job and somewhere to live. Having made this momentous resolution my despair evaporated into elation. The week prior to Christmas I worked for the Post Office sorting office to earn some money for the impending arrival of my baby. *My* baby – how good that sounded.

Two days before Christmas I went with Jean to collect him. He was almost unrecognisable from the tiny infant I'd left just six weeks previously, three pounds heavier and much more alert. "There, you hold him," his foster mum offered him up, beaming, delighted to see mother and son reunited. "I'll miss him, but we'll be getting another in the New Year," she said happily. I looked down at his sweet expression, his eyes no longer oriental-looking, more like mine, and as he gazed back at me a smile seemed to flicker across his face. It felt so good to be holding him once more and I bent to smell his head, inhaling the heady elixir.

The foster mum proceeded to give me instructions on how to care for my baby – how to prepare his bottles, change his nappies and bathe him. He was so much bigger, his routine different from the hospital one. Jean sat and watched *Lassie Come Home* on the TV, totally uninterested in the art of baby care. We bid fond farewells to his foster mother and she waved 'goodbye' as we drove away. Throughout the drive home he was well-behaved, comforted by the car's movement. On arrival in his new residence, however, his wails began to fill the air and we rushed around assembling bottles and mixing up feeds. In the hospital it had been easy with everything already prepared – our inexperience and lack of confidence were conveyed to my poor baby, who developed tummy ache. This continued over the Christmas holiday until driven to distraction by his constant cries, I phoned the doctor. "It sounds like wind to me. Probably the teat is too small or too large. You'll need to experiment and rub his back to wind him during and after his feed," he advised. We spent frantic hours rubbing his back with little effect, until finally, in desperation we added a nip of whisky to his bottle – it was New Year after all! This ancient remedy, handed down from our Scottish granny, resulted in four long, blissful hours of silence – only spoiled by our guilt at what we'd done to one so small, hoping that we hadn't irretrievably damaged his tiny liver. A wicker clothes basket was his bed as we didn't have a cot. It wasn't long before I mastered the art of baby care, and once I'd enlarged the hole in the teat with a darning needle, the newly named Sean became a lovable and contented child, only crying when he was hungry and sleeping through the night, much to our relief.

Soon after New Year I received a letter from Maria, my Italian girlfriend in Glasgow. I ripped it open and read it avidly, becoming particularly excited when she wrote, *'You'll never guess who I bumped into at the disco Friday night – Duncan! We had quite a chat and he seemed to be feeling guilty about you and the baby.'* My heart burst with joy, and filled with hope for a reunion and with my new motherly feelings I wrote to him saying that I'd decided to keep our son and enclosed a photo of proud mum plus baby. I ended this missive, *' If you'd like to see him please contact me at my sister's address.'* He never replied to this letter, much to my disappointment, but I was too preoccupied with Sean to dwell upon it.

As the dark, drab days of January dragged by I became increasingly dissatisfied and bored. Sean slept when he wasn't feeding or bathing, giving me time to brood over my situation, wondering what the future had in store. He was growing rapidly and I had to get a cot when I noticed the wickerwork impression on his head – he was too big for the clothes basket! There was no word from the Children's Officer but we were also looking at the local paper. One day Jean spotted an advertisement. "Look at this, Margaret, someone's searching for a nanny and it's a local address." The idea of becoming a nanny didn't thrill me, but thinking, *nothing ventured, nothing gained,* I replied. To my surprise a letter came by return post asking me to come for interview – the surprise was because I'd mentioned that I was an unmarried mother of eighteen with a two-month-old son.

On the way to the address Jean and I imagined a palatial residence with luxurious furnishings as surely only wealthy people could afford a live-in nanny, a bit like the Queen. Imagine our amazement when we realised that it was only a small flat. We were even more taken aback when the woman who answered the door appeared ordinarily dressed, like us. No diamonds or furs to be seen. Her round, pleasant face was framed by long, wavy brown hair and she welcomed us warmly. "Come in, come in out of the cold," she said, leading the way into a far from spacious sitting room. A lean, dark-haired, swarthy-looking man was sitting on a chair, cutting his toe nails. She frowned slightly at him, "This is my husband, Bob. Oh, and I'm Cathy, by the way."

"Pleased to meet you, Cathy," replied Jean, trying to ignore Bob, although by this time he'd put down his nail clippers. Jean looked harder at Cathy. "You look familiar – haven't I seen you somewhere before?"

"Well, I sing at the local folk club," Cathy responded.

"Of course, that's it! We've been there a few times, haven't we Margaret? It's a great place with good folk music."

Bob chimed in, "Yes, the beer's good too."

Cathy continued, "We're very pleased you replied to our ad, Margaret. You've got a baby son, you said?"

"Yes, I have. His name's Sean and he's very good," I told her, hoping that my son wouldn't pose a problem. We'd left him in Ken's tender care, sound asleep in his cot.

"Oh, I think he'll be company for our boys," she said. *Boys, what does she mean? In the ad it said there was only one child*, I thought. She noticed my puzzled expression. "Yes, I'm afraid I twisted the truth slightly in the ad. We've got twin boys of one-year-old, and it's impossible to find anybody willing to look after them." Jean and I sat, trying to absorb this information. Cathy got up and announced, "I think you should meet them. They're amusing themselves in their play pen next door." We followed her into the boys' room where they were happily playing with their toys. When they saw us they both struggled to their feet and stood, holding onto the side of the pen, surveying us silently with wide eyes. They were adorable and non-identical: one had big, brown eyes and brown, curly hair, the other large, grey eyes and straight, black hair.

Jean gushed, "They're lovely and so well behaved!"

Cathy interrupted, "They're not always so angelic. You should see them earlier in the day, crawling all over the place and walking around, holding onto the furniture. It won't be long until they're properly walking – that'll be fun!" My mind reeled, *yes, fun all right, with Sean to look after as well.* I couldn't visualise how I'd cope. Cathy detected my concern. "If you decide to take the position you may come here a few times a week first, to get the hang of their routine. That way you'll know if you'll be able to do it, which I'm sure you will," she told me confidently.

We returned to the sitting room where Bob offered us a cup of tea, adding, "We're moving to the south of England shortly because we've both got jobs there. We'll go as soon as the buying of our house is completed." *I don't want to move back south,* I thought.

Cathy continued enthusiastically, "The house is large enough for all of us. You'll have your own room and later Sean can either share with the boys, or there's a box room he might like."

"That sounds fine," I said, still uncertain.

There was no stopping Cathy now, though. I'd told her about my interrupted studies in my application and she'd obviously been thinking about it. "We'd be willing to babysit while you attend night classes to keep up with your studies. You're a bright girl and I'm sure you don't want to be a nanny forever," she chuckled sympathetically. *They both seem really nice and kind and the boys are lovely. Maybe I'll give it a try.*

I looked at Jean, searching for support. "Well, what do you think, Margaret?" she placed responsibility for a decision on me.

I took the plunge, "I'd like to accept the position and I'll come and get to know the boys, like you suggested."

"That's great!" Cathy and Bob exclaimed in unison.

*

Over the next month I became more acquainted with the twins and their routine. I'd arrive first thing in the morning with Sean, when they'd just woken up. This was the part I least enjoyed. Their nappies were sodden and my eyes stung as ammoniac fumes hit them. Once changed I gave them breakfast. This was accomplished by seating them side by side in their high chairs, offering spoonfuls of cereal to first one and then the other. They were in perfect co-ordination, contentedly regarding each other as they fed. Sean slotted into their programme happily. He loved to sit, propped up with cushions, watching them playing and listening to their gurgling attempts at communication. I was becoming used to the idea of being in this role of nanny for a while, but Cathy and Bob's move kept being postponed, they were having such difficulty with their house purchase. I began to despair that the re-location would ever happen and felt that my life was on hold.

Seventeen

One day in February the Children's Officer came to visit. "Margaret, I've been notified that a man living in Edinburgh is looking for a housekeeper. Would you be interested?"

My heart rate increased expectantly. *I'd much prefer to be in Edinburgh.* "Yes, I would be interested," I answered.

"That's good. He sounds respectable and has excellent references. He's a widower with two sons of primary school age and has no objection to a young baby, with plenty of space in his home. He has his own building business and lives in a pleasant part of the city."

This all sounded great to me and she handed over his address and phone number, which she'd been clutching tightly in her hand. "Good luck, Margaret. Please let me know how you get on," she said smiling as she left.

For several evenings I tried to phone him from the call box down the road, with no success, so I wrote instead. A few days later I received a telegram – *yes, a telegram!* 'Please contact me immediately about the vacancy – Matthew Gillespie,' I read, filled with excitement. In my limited experience telegrams were solely reserved for communicating deaths and disasters: it must surely be an eccentric, and possibly wealthy man, who would act in this way. My imagination, having had little to feed it for so long, ran riot. *Maybe it would be like the tumultuous relationship between Jane Eyre and Mr Rochester? Or the nun turned governess in the Sound of Music – that was SO romantic!* I put on Jean's *Sound of Music* album and danced around, singing the song, *'I Have Confidence'* :

> *I've always longed for adventure*
> *To do the things I've never dared*
> *And here I'm facing adventure*
> *Then why am I so scared*
> *A captain (builder) with seven (two) children*
> *What's so fearsome about that?*

When Jean came home from work I told her excitedly about the telegram. "Sounds a bit frantic," she grimaced, "but I guess you'd better phone him. I'll chum you to the call box."

He answered the phone immediately. " I'm glad you got my telegram, Margaret. Would it be possible for you to come down, say next weekend, and stay over Saturday night?"

Oh, I'm not sure about that – but I suppose it's a long way to go for one day. "I guess that's okay. I'll be coming by train and will let you know the time later."

"Don't worry, I can check that out – there's probably only one morning train from Inverness. I'll meet you at the station with my car."

He sounds a bit too keen. "That's very kind of you. How will we recognise each other?"

"Well, I'll be carrying a rolled-up copy of *The Times*," he responded, "joking, of course. I'm tall and rather handsome, so I've been told, in my late thirties and will be wearing a brown, woollen jacket and black cords.

What about you? I presume you won't be bringing your baby?"

I hadn't thought about Sean. *Oh dear, I'll have to leave him with Jean, but will she be able to cope?* "Just a minute, I'll need to ask my sister if she'll look after him," I cried, hoping that I didn't sound too panic-stricken. After a hurried conversation poor Jean reluctantly agreed to be a substitute 'mum' the following weekend. I picked up the receiver, "Yes, that's okay. I'm tall and slim with short, wavy brown hair and glasses." I frenziedly decided what to wear, " Oh, and I'll be dressed in a long, maroon woollen skirt and a black coat."

"Okay, I reckon that's enough of a description. See you on Saturday," he responded and rang off.

I was busy feeding Sean the next day when the doorbell rang. It was another telegram. I tore it open and read, *'My present elderly housekeeper has just fallen ill, and she won't be back. Would you be able to start immediately? Matthew Gillespie.'* I felt flustered – *why this sudden haste? He hadn't mentioned this housekeeper on the phone.* I would have to phone him from the wretched phone box again.

"Hello, Mr Gillespie, it's Margaret. I'm afraid I can't begin work right now."

He interrupted, "Oh, please Margaret. I'm in a terrible pickle! The boys need someone here when they come home from school and the house is in a dreadful state."

I didn't like the sound of this at all. "I'm sorry, but I'd rather meet you first before making a decision," I said firmly. Sounding harassed he reluctantly agreed with me, saying that he'd meet me on Saturday.

*

Saturday arrived, and filled with trepidation about meeting this strange man who indulged in the sending of erratic telegrams, I boarded the Edinburgh train. Sean was left in the not very capable hands of Jean. I'd drawn up a long list of all the minute details involved in baby minding – meal times, how to concoct his feeds, nappy changing and bathing routine, hoping that he'd survive the ordeal.

At Edinburgh Waverley Station we eventually recognised each other in the crowd. His description of himself was, in my opinion, not entirely accurate. He seemed too old, too short and not handsome enough, all of which had a dampening effect upon my fantasies. "You must be Margaret," he said, holding out his hand, shaking mine too hard. "My car's over there. It's the white BMW," he continued and I followed him to his flashy vehicle. I clambered in, secretly admiring the plush interior, while we chatted about the weather and similar safe subjects.

After about half-an-hour he came to a halt on the driveway of his house. It was a large, detached bungalow, with another building in the sizeable garden. "That's my office," he commented as we got out of the car, "it's handy to work from home, although I'm out a lot checking up on my builders." *Oh, so he doesn't get his hands dirty – he's the big boss,* I realised.

We went inside the house, which was spacious and pleasantly furnished. It didn't look untidy – *he must've found somebody to clean up, thank goodness.* "Come and meet my boys," he said, leading the way into the lounge where they were sitting on the settee, watching television. They were so engrossed in a cowboy film that they hardly looked up. "Boys, this is Margaret, who may be coming to look after us," my possible employer explained. This got their attention and they looked at me with wary expressions. "This is Calum, he's the oldest at nine," he tousled his son's thick, brown hair, "and this wee imp's Fergus – he's seven." Fergus's blue eyes stared at me through a mass of fair curls, unsmiling, scratching at his hands.

"Hello boys, pleased to meet you," I said politely and they replied in unison, "pleased to meet you too." With that they turned their attention back to the TV screen.

Matthew led the way to the kitchen. "Don't mind the boys," he told me, "they've had a string of housekeepers, I'm afraid, and it's unsettled them, especially Fergus." He showed me all the kitchen gadgets and then the rest of the house. When we reached his bedroom he announced, "This is the bridal suite," and laughed heartily. I felt uneasy but dismissed it as a rather strange joke from this somewhat eccentric man. My room, should I accept, was at the front of the bungalow with plenty of space for Sean to sleep. "Well, what do you think of my abode?" he asked, and I replied that it was very comfortable, which seemed to please him. "Can you picture yourself living here?" he persisted.

"Yes, maybe," I answered vaguely.

"I hope this 'maybe' will become 'certainly'," he uttered, fixing me with a blue-eyed stare, not dissimilar to his son's. "I'll away and make the tea now," he continued, "you sit with the boys. Maybe they'll chat with you when I'm not around," he chuckled and disappeared into the kitchen.

It was a relief to be relieved of conversing with him and I became as engrossed in the film as the boys.

Cooking odours wafted into the room and I realised that I was hungry, although it didn't smell too appetising. Our 'chef' appeared at the door. "Tea's ready! Come on boys, time to turn off the telly." They meekly acquiesced and trooped into the kitchen where the table was already laid. "I like good, plain Scottish food," Matthew informed me, as he dished out plates of mince and tatties, without any sign of fresh vegetables. *How dull,* I thought, eating the virtually tasteless yet edible meal. *He's put no onions, garlic or herbs in this,* I registered. *Well, that'll need to change!*

After our meal we did the dishes together – *this is homely,* I decided. As he washed up he told me a little more about his situation. "Since my wife died of cancer three years ago I've had a succession of housekeepers, which has upset the boys, as I said. I desperately want someone who'll stay, so that they can feel more secure." I found myself sympathising with him and began to warm to him more as the evening wore on. After we'd finished clearing up we returned to the lounge. "Boys, you sit on the floor so that Margaret and I can have the settee," he ordered, motioning me to sit beside him, although there were two armchairs to choose from. *I suppose I'd better do as I'm told.* I would have preferred one of the armchairs, and felt under pressure. We settled ourselves on the settee, with the children crouched together on the floor in front of us. Looking at me sorrowfully Matthew observed, "I've got into the habit of keeping the boys up late, just to keep me company." I felt sorry for him and he edged closer to me, attempting to put his arm round me. *What on earth's he thinking of? Especially with his sons here!* Hastily I moved further away. Then he addressed the boys, "Right, it's time for bed you two." They left the room unwillingly, with Matthew shooing them off eagerly.

While 'my employer' was busy settling the children I remained sitting on the couch wondering how to cope with this tricky situation. Despite my fantasies I'd never dreamt that he'd be expecting me to be anything more than a housekeeper, after all the Children's Officer had described him as 'respectable, with excellent references,' so surely this must be so? But was I that naïve?

He soon finished putting the boys to bed and returned to sit close beside me on the settee. Once again he put his arm around me. My heart began to thump wildly – *what am I going to do?* I managed to stammer, "This doesn't seem right, Matthew – we haven't known each other for long enough, and anyway, I thought it was just a housekeeper you needed."

I tried to move away but had reached the edge of the sofa. I was trapped. He moved even closer and whispered softly in my ear, "Margaret, I'm a normal man; I'm very lonely and I need a woman – please forgive me." His whispering did strange things to my insides, which had almost forgotten what it was like to feel such sensations, so I let him kiss me. Finally I allowed him to lead me to the 'bridal suite' – the 'joke' having been made in truth, not jest.

He quickly undressed motioning me to do the same, which I did, reluctantly. Leaving on my underclothes I rapidly joined him in his king-sized bed. I shivered under the cold sheets and he pulled me to him, removing my bra and pants expertly, covering my bare flesh with kisses. *This doesn't feel right.* There'd been no alcohol to relax me and I felt awkward and out of place, while this man, almost a stranger, explored my body. He did at least use a condom and was soon satisfied, rolling off of me and instantly falling asleep, snoring lightly. I was completely turned-off and crept into my room to escape and sleep.

In the morning he drove me to the station, having offered me the job. No doubt I'd passed the interview with flying colours: I was to start on Tuesday, so great was his need for a 'housekeeper'.

Eighteen

Jean met me at Inverness station and immediately asked me how my visit had been. "Oh, I got the job and he wants me to begin on Tuesday."

She looked intently at my face. "He must be desperate, are you sure you want to do this?" She deluged me with questions about him which I tried to dodge, but finally she prised the weekend's events out of me. She was shocked. "So much for the Social Work Department's recommendation. He's a rogue and has probably behaved similarly with all those other housekeepers."

"Hmm. I suppose you're right," I replied, "but at least it's a job, and in Edinburgh, where I really want to live. It'll give me time to sort myself out and find something better."

"Well, if that's what you want to do . . ." she left it hanging and proceeded to tell me all about Sean, who had been well-behaved throughout my absence.

I contacted Cathy and Bob about my new position. *'I'm sorry but I'd rather remain in Scotland,'* I wrote, continuing, *'hopefully you'll be able to find someone suitable before you move.'*

They weren't too happy about this, and replied, *'Are you certain about this, Margaret? We'll leave our position open in case your job in Edinburgh ends in disaster.'* How on earth could that happen?

*

After a frantic day of packing I was back at Waverley Station, complete with Sean, his pram and my enormous trunk – how I managed all this luggage single-handedly, I cannot remember. Matthew had succeeded in finding a porter to wheel my trunk along while I followed with Sean, who was enjoying all the frenzied station activity from the comfort of his pram.

Once he had installed me in his home, Matthew went back to work leaving me to settle in. The boys returned from school and I welcomed them as best I could. "Hello boys. How was your day at school?" They mumbled something unintelligible, then Fergus piped up, "Have you brought us any sweeties?"

Oh dear, I should've thought of that. "Sorry, Fergus but I didn't have time. I'll get you some tomorrow," I said lamely.

Fergus was used to disappointment. "Okay, Smarties are my favourite," he responded philosophically. I gave them some milk and biscuits and then Calum disappeared into his room. Fergus hung around, keen to chat. Without any prompting he began to talk about his father. "You know my mummy ran away and left him and she took my little sister." *Surely that can't be true?* My mind reeled in shock.

The little boy was sitting at the kitchen table, scratching his hands again, his face pale and anxious. *The poor wee thing.* Clumsily I asked, "But I thought your mummy had died?"

He gazed at me with his sad, blue eyes, twisting a golden curl with his fingers. "Yes, she did die, but then daddy married someone else and got my baby sister, Susan."

Well, some of it's true, at least. "Oh, I see. Do you miss her?" *What a stupid question!*

"Yes. I miss her all the time and my step-mum. She was kind and bought me lots of Smarties." I felt sorry for him, but also manipulated. He was obviously disturbed and had developed skills designed to produce sympathy and sweeties. I turned on the TV and we watched the children's programmes together – it was safer than continuing the conversation.

My boss had instructed me to make mince and tatties (*again!*) for tea, which I did, noting that the cupboards were devoid of any ingredients to add to it, except salt and pepper. He ate it with gusto, remarking, "You make fine mince 'n tatties, Margaret." I tried not to grimace as I ate the tasteless meal and vowed to buy some flavourings as soon as possible.

As it was a week night the boys went to bed early and I supervised their bedtime activities. Sean by then was sleeping through the night after his evening bottle. Fergus still needed some help with bathing and I was shocked to see patches of ugly, red eczema on his skin. *That's why he keeps scratching his hands,* I realised as I saw their cracked surface. "Do you put any cream on these sore bits," I asked and he nodded and pointed to the bathroom cabinet. Once he was dry I carefully rubbed the cream onto his sensitive skin, then put him to bed and read a story to him and Calum, who was already in his pyjamas.

"Please leave the night light on," Calum instructed as I shut the door.

Matthew settled in front of the TV, leaving me to do the dishes alone. Afterwards I joined him on the settee and began to interrogate him. "Fergus was telling me about your wife and daughter running away – is this true?" I glared at him, anger bubbling just below the surface.

He shifted nervously in his seat, averting his eyes. "Yes, I'm afraid it is true, but I *was* a widower, you know."

"Yes, I know – your son told me, but that doesn't alter the fact that you deceived me and the Social Work Department," I retorted angrily.

He was looking at me now. "Well, I couldn't tell them about that, could I? It would've jeopardised my chance of getting a young housekeeper with a baby, wouldn't it?"

I was flabbergasted. "It certainly would've! They'd have thought you had an ulterior motive – which you had."

"Please don't think too badly of me, Margaret. I've been through a terrible time with my dear wife dying of cancer and then losing my second wife and daughter." *If you think you're going to get my sympathy, you're mistaken.*

I retaliated, "And why did they run away from you? You must've done something really bad."

"No, no, I didn't, honestly. She was one of my housekeepers, a money-grabbing bitch. She didn't love me, just my money, but she won't be getting any."

Now he's showing his true colours all right. "I don't like this. I'm going to leave as soon as possible," I stated.

"Oh, please don't go, Margaret. I'm not a bad man and the boys couldn't bear another upheaval so soon. Please stay." He looked imploringly at me.

The sight of this rich and powerful man reduced to a pathetic beggar, affected me strangely. *Where can I go, except back to Jean's? Maybe I should try and stay a little longer?* I found myself saying, "Okay, Matthew, I'll stay." He was suitably grateful and clasped me to him, covering my face with kisses, which naturally resulted in an excursion to the 'bridal suite', where our differences were temporarily appeased.

After this rude awakening to the sordidness of the situation I became increasingly more depressed as the days passed by. Nothing that I did seemed to be right – my tasty meals were too flavoursome for his taste buds. He began to make his own dull dinners, while I ate earlier with the boys, who preferred fish fingers and sausages. There was also a daily help who did the housework and washing, which left me little to do, apart from looking after Sean and the boys when they came home from school.

Another job I had was to answer the phone, which rang incessantly throughout the day. I had to record all the messages correctly for his attention in the evening. "What's this number here? I can hardly read it, and what exactly did they want?" he'd ask irritably, and I'd stutter something incomprehensible. "Really, Margaret, the least you can do is record these messages clearly – I don't ask you to do much."

Matthew went out many nights: where I did not know, but he'd return rather drunk and come creeping into my room. "Margaret, Margaret, wake up," he'd say, shaking my shoulder. "Please come to bed with me," he'd cajole, breathing boozy fumes into my ear. I felt frightened of him in that condition and meekly climbed into his bed, where he relieved himself with little regard for my pleasure, although he was careful not to get me pregnant. Afterwards, as he lay snoring, I'd creep back to the safety of my bed, unable to sleep for many hours.

*

An old school friend of mine had moved to Edinburgh with her parents, and in an effort to cheer myself up I visited them on one of my days off. I hadn't told them about Sean, so when my friend's mum opened the door and saw the pram, she gasped, "Oh, Margaret – I didn't know you'd had a baby."

"I had him on the fifth of November. His name's Sean," I told her as she led the way into their lounge, where my friend was sitting watching TV.

Before she could say anything her mum gushed, "You'll never guess, Vicky, Margaret's got a baby son."

"What a surprise – why didn't you tell me?" Vicky turned off the TV to fully concentrate on me. "Where is he?"

"He's outside sleeping in his pram," I answered, trying to work out how to explain his sudden appearance.

Vicky's mum came to the rescue, "Would you like a cup of tea?"

"Yes, that'd be lovely," I replied, steering the conversation around to their lives. But it wasn't long before my whole sorry tale was told. They both seemed very understanding about it and I was invited to stay for tea. They fussed over Sean, who'd woken up and was being his usual charming self.

Vicky cradled him in her arms, gazing fondly at his face. "He's gorgeous, and so good. Look, he's smiling at me," she said, tickling his chin, while her mum looked on, equally enthralled.

On leaving Vicky said, "You must come again, Margaret. Phone me any time," and they both stood at their gate, waving as I pushed Sean down the road.

A couple of days later I received a letter from Vicky's father. *'Dear Margaret,'* I read, *'my wife and daughter were most upset by your recent visit and I forbid you to ever contact them again.' How can he write this? They seemed so pleased to see me and Sean.* I was distressed by their rejection, which was the second I'd received. One of my aunts had written coldly, without compassion, stating that she and her husband wanted nothing more to do with me. Apart from this particular aunt, all my other relatives had responded sympathetically to my news (except for Mum and Jim).

*

My first week as Matthew's 'housekeeper' ended; my depression deepened and I wrote to the couple with twins, hoping that they'd be able to offer me the job again. They replied, *'Sorry, Margaret, but we've been lucky enough to find another girl who's willing to tackle the task of looking after our twins and we feel that we cannot let her down. We hope you understand and wish you success in your future life.'*

With this news I sank into the depths of despair, and being so near to Glasgow my thoughts began to turn once more to Sean's father. My relatives had persuaded me to see a lawyer, one of my aunts writing, *'He shouldn't be allowed to get away with ruining your life, Margaret.'* Initially I'd wanted to be totally independent, but gradually I'd changed my mind as I realised how difficult it was raising Sean alone. However, with all the turmoil I'd done nothing about it.

The situation with Matthew deteriorated rapidly as

the second week began. He started to develop paranoid feelings about my presence in his home. One evening once the boys were in bed he sat beside me on the settee – something he hadn't done since the night I'd moved in. "Margaret, I need to talk to you." *Oh dear, this sounds ominous.* He went on, "My wife has written to me and she said she'd engaged a detective to find out whether I'm being unfaithful to her."

"What! You must be joking."

"No, Margaret, I'm not. She left me so that puts her in an insecure position to obtain grounds for divorce on her terms. I told you, she's a money-grabber and if she can obtain evidence that I'm being unfaithful, it'll make her case stronger." *What a nincompoop! He should have thought of that when he engaged a young, unmarried mother to be his housekeeper.*

After this proclamation, he rarely invited me into the 'bridal suite'. When he could stand the strain no longer he went to enormous lengths – checking the outside of the house for snoopers, tightly closing the curtains and whispering conspiratorially to me as action commenced. Finally he announced, "I'm afraid, Margaret, that you'll have to leave as your presence here could give incriminating evidence to that bitch." I couldn't understand the sheer stupidity of the man.

"I've got nowhere to go except back to my sister's, which I don't want to do."

He looked at me with sympathy but nevertheless stated, "I'm sorry, but I'd like you to leave by the end of next week." *Oh, no – what am I going to do?*

Nineteen

I was tired, miserable and desperate, so I phoned Duncan. For once luck was with me, as he answered the phone. It was heaven to hear his voice again and I immediately launched into a confused account of my predicament. He seemed concerned and said, "Why dinnae you come ower tae Glesga the morra, as it's Saturday? You can meet ma parents – mibbe they'll be able tae help."

Temporarily elated I prepared for the journey, which entailed organising all the paraphernalia required by Sean for this important trip to meet his grandparents. There were no other housekeeping positions available, according to the Social Work Department, and I was wary of accepting a similar post with an unattached male. All my hopes were focused on this meeting with Duncan's parents – *'please let them love Sean,'* I prayed.

The following afternoon I boarded the Glasgow train, complete with Sean, who was fast becoming a seasoned traveller. On arrival at the station I took a taxi to Duncan's parents' house. His mum was home alone and gave me an unexpectedly warm welcome. "Hello Margaret, come away in – it's sae cold ootside," she said, ushering me into the lounge where a fire was burning cosily. I remembered that other occasion when I'd been passionately embraced by Duncan on the rug beside it, and tried to push it from my mind.

"I'll need to get my son," I told her and manoeuvred Sean and his pram into the hallway.

She bent down and peeped inside. Sean was wide awake, taking in his new surroundings. "Och, whit a bonnie bairn," cooed his grandma, which was sweet music to my ears.

"I'll take him out as he'll be needing his bottle soon."

"Of course. Ah'll put the kettle oan fur hot water." She busied herself in the kitchen while I unpacked Sean's things. I was feeding him when Duncan's dad arrived home from work.

"Please dinnae get up," he said and introduced himself. Duncan didn't look like either of his parents, I pondered, wondering if he was adopted.

Duncan's mum appeared. "Tea's ready. Please come away in tae the dining room, Margaret." I put Sean back in his pram where he fell asleep, full of milk.

Once we were seated at the table, Duncan's mum announced, " Duncan's working late taenight but he'll come 'n see you later at the hotel we've booked fur you." *Why have they done this? Surely there's space for us here?*

Noting my puzzled expression Duncan's father explained, "Oor lawyer advised us tae reserve a hotel fur yous. He said that if we put yous up fur a night we'd be admitting Duncan's paternity an' it could be used as evidence against him if you were thinking o' takin' him tae court."

I shifted uneasily in my chair, aware of their eyes, which were fixed upon me. There was nothing I could say, their initial warm welcome was fast evaporating as they voiced their increasing doubt that Duncan was

Sean's father. "He doesnae look like Duncan," they agreed. This was indeed true as he was the living image of myself.

I had to say something. "Well, he's not even four months old and it's difficult to see a likeness at that age, although he does look like me."

"Hmm. We're extremely worried that you might decide tae gae tae court. It'd be the death o' his granny," Duncan's dad confided.

"I've hardly had time to think about it," I said, "and I haven't even seen a lawyer."

They looked somewhat relieved, but his dad continued, "Ma mother's auld 'n frail an' it'd probably be in all the papers, the local ones at least, sae we couldnae keep it secret." *Surely they're exaggerating? There must be loads of paternity suits in a big city like Glasgow.*

His father went on, "We were wondering if you'd be interested in a lump sum payment, tae keep it oot o' court?" *They want to buy me off!* I was completely overwhelmed by their proposal.

"I don't know because I thought Duncan might want to marry me, but if he doesn't I suppose that'd be okay." I couldn't think straight – it was all too much to take in.

*

Eventually they drove me to the hotel and invited me to return for lunch the following day. Duncan arrived at ten, no doubt having been for a few pints after work to fortify himself in preparation for this gruelling encounter. On entering the room he glanced awkwardly at his small offspring, who lay innocently sleeping through this important meeting between his young and foolish parents. He made no attempt to kiss me and sat down on a large armchair in the corner of the room, an expression of vague dismay on his face. We made small talk for a while and then he said, avoiding my eyes, "I suppose we could live taegither fur a time, tae see if things work oot." I noted his lack of enthusiasm and this affected me. I could suddenly picture myself alone each evening, with only Sean for company, while he was in the pub with his mates. We were both uncertain of our feelings for each other, but nevertheless after two hours of talking we decided to find a flat in Glasgow together. As he left he pecked me hurriedly on the cheek, plainly relieved to be going.

It was just me and his mum at lunch the next day. Duncan and his dad were working overtime. I told her about our plans – she didn't seem too happy about it. As I had nowhere to go until we found a flat, which would probably be tricky with a young baby, I asked her if we could stay with them temporarily until we were settled. "Och, Margaret, I need tae ask Duncan an' his da whit they think aboot this when they git in frae work taenight."

"Okay. I'm returning to Edinburgh this afternoon to pack up my belongings," I said, with little expectation of anything positive happening.

"Awright. I'll phone you this evening," she replied.

I was back in Edinburgh in time for tea and was greeted with pleasure by Matthew and his sons, which surprised me under the circumstances. "We've missed you, haven't we boys?" my employer said, without a hint of sarcasm.

Soon after our meal Duncan's mother phoned as promised. "I'm afraid Duncan's sulking in his room,

Margaret. Ah'll try an' git him tae contact you later."

A couple of hours passed and then he phoned, sounding in a very bad mood. Obviously, the prospect of living with me and Sean was not filling him with delight. At length, after much persuasion, he agreed that the only course I could adopt would be to move to Glasgow. "I'll phone you aboot the final arrangements in a day or two," he promised.

At bedtime Matthew was in a romantic mood. "Please come to my room, Margaret," he said enticingly. "Perhaps we can work something out so that you can stay after all." *Oh, yeah – I don't believe a word you say.* I was getting used to his constant changes of temperament and was greeted at breakfast by a very different man. "I'm afraid you'll have to go, Margaret cos your presence here will upset my divorce."

"That's okay, Matthew. I've decided to move to Glasgow anyway."

*

A few days later Duncan phoned. "Hi, Margaret. I'm afraid ma folks will nae let yous stay here."

"What do you mean? Your mum seemed okay about it." I was losing any hope of a reconciliation.

"Och, I guess it wis ma da. He's worried aboot you goin' tae court."

I interrupted, "But I thought we were going to live together? I wouldn't be taking you to court then."

He sighed deeply. "We've taken the advice o' oor lawyer. He says we should all hae a blood test which could disprove ma paternity."

"But I told you I was certain you're the father."

"I ken, but ah dinnae believe you." His voice sounded cold and distant.

"Okay, I'll have the test, then you'll see."

"Unfortunately it cannae positively identify if I'm the father, but it can definitely disprove it."

This was all news to me. DNA testing had yet to be discovered. "Oh, I see. Anyway, where am I going to stay – in the hotel?"

"Nae, we cannae afford that. They've foond yous a place in a hame fur unmarried mothers."

I slowly absorbed this bombshell. "Oh! That's so kind of them," I said sarcastically.

"I'm sorry, but that's all they're prepared tae dae." His tone had softened somewhat. "I'll meet yous at the train station the morra afternoon, aroond two o'clock, okay?" I could think of no better alternative and reluctantly agreed to go to the home.

The next day was Saturday and I sadly packed my trunk, which was becoming worn with all the moving around. Matthew drove me to the station and helped me and Sean onto the train. "Please keep in touch, Margaret, if you decide to return to Edinburgh."

"Yes, I will. I'm going to look for another position here, if possible."

"That's good. I'm really sorry it had to end this way," he admitted. He waved as the train pulled out of the station and I realised that my dominant emotion was one of pity for him.

Twenty

As the train arrived in Glasgow I remembered the excitement and happiness I'd felt on the first occasion. So much had happened in such a short time, changing my life dramatically. Duncan greeted me with little enthusiasm and quickly drove me to the home, which wasn't far from the city centre. Dropping me there he remarked, "The blood test has been arranged an' ah dinnae want tae huv any contact wi' you until we ken the result." *This is the lawyer speaking, not him.* I sadly watched him drive away after his chilling announcement, then turned towards the house. It was an old, rambling, stone-built place, in need of a coat of paint.

A woman dressed in a blue overall, with short, greying hair and hazel eyes came out to meet me. "Ya must be Margaret," she said kindly, " 'n this wee one is yur son, Sean." I agreed that this was so as she led the way up a flight of stone steps to the dirty-brown front door. "Has Mr MacCallum telt ya anything aboot us?"

It seemed strange to hear Duncan's father's name in this setting. "No, I'm afraid he hasn't," I was forced to admit.

"Please sit doon." She pointed to a hard chair opposite her desk. "The hame's run by the Church o' Scotland 'n we huv strict rules. There are ten lassies here the noo. Two huv just had their weans, while the others are all pregnant. We dinnae really cater fur weans as auld as yurs." *Duncan's dad pleaded my case extremely well,* I thought wryly.

She went on, "The lassies are nae allowed oot after 6pm. They must be punctual fur meals 'n tak' part in the dish washing rota. It's lights oot at 11pm. If ya need tae feed yur wean in the night ya may switch oan a night light. The lassies wi' weans are kept in a separate room sae as no tae disturb the pregnant ones. Visitors are restricted tae daytime only 'n must be met in the lounge. The weans' fathers are discouraged frae visiting – we dinnae want any trouble." *Oh dear, it sounds like prison.* I determined to leave the place as soon as possible.

Once settled in the home I began to arrange my future life. The first place I visited was the local Social Security office. I was forced to wait for hours, despite having Sean with me; the seemingly endless queue of people moved slowly forward, all looking equally dowdy, with identical forlorn, listless expressions on their faces. Some grey-faced old men with stubbly chins, their tatty overcoats trailing to the floor, their battered, black boots with bits of string for shoelaces, were enjoying their wait. They swigged at unlabelled bottles, alcoholic fumes wafting around the room, mixing with the heady aroma of unwashed bodies, stale tobacco smoke and disinfectant.

Eventually it was my turn to be interviewed. I approached the counter with relief, clutching Sean, who was now becoming noisy and restless, demanding his lunch. After an interminable interrogation, during which countless forms were filled in, I was told to sit down and await payment. Finally I received a brown paper envelope containing just enough money to live on for a week. Putting it safely in my pocket, I hurried out into the fresh air.

On my return to the home I gave Sean his lunch, which he gulped down frantically after his long and tedious morning, then changed his nappy, which was in a foul state. Clean and fed we ventured back out to the legal aid office, who sent me to a lawyer. He listened carefully to all the details of the case, then said, "A lump sum settlement could certainly be arranged legally, but we'll have to wait for the blood test result and then hope that the MacCallums won't change their minds."

This news invigorated me to plan for the future. I had to accept that marriage to Duncan would result in disaster: we were both too young to make a commitment and would grow to resent each other as the years went by. Sean was probably better off fatherless and who knew what the future might bring? I hoped that with the money I could afford to buy a small flat, and then I could find a job. After that one visit to a Social Security office I had no desire to repeat it. I'd felt humiliated after the hostile interview.

The home had a lot of information about bringing up a child on your own. The Children's Officer in Inverness had led me to believe that the only way I could keep my son was to get a housekeeping post. She'd never mentioned nursery schools, either through neglect or ignorance. At the home I learned that councils ran nursery schools, where single mums' children from birth to school age were given priority. They were free and open from 8am to 6pm. I felt a weight shift from my mind – with the money to buy a flat, a nursery place and a job I'd be totally independent and could even start studying again.

My next visit was to the Employment Exchange, who

made an appointment at the Occupational Guidance centre. When they heard about my situation they were kind and considerate and asked me to complete a long questionnaire in order to discover which career would suit me best. They suggested the scientific Civil Service, or psychiatric nursing, as my interests and qualifications were scientifically based. I could not return to Auchincruive because I needed an income and there was no nursery provision there. I'd decided to return to Edinburgh to settle – Glasgow had too many unpleasant memories and Edinburgh was more appealing to me. Once there I'd investigate job opportunities.

*

My immediate future was still unsettled. I could not remain at the home for long and the lump sum settlement would take several months to complete. This meant that the only course open to me was to find another housekeeping position in Edinburgh until the money was available to buy a flat. I placed an advertisement in the Edinburgh Evening News, stating: *Young mother plus baby looking for a housekeeping position – anything considered.* I placed the home's phone number at the end of it.

The ad went in for three nights and the first night I received five calls, two of which were from women. I arranged to see them on the following Saturday, leaving Sean in the tender care of the girls in the home, who were only too willing to look after him for a day. The women that ran the home, however, were not so sympathetic to my plans. I was summoned to the office, where the chief woman sat glowering at me. "Well, Margaret, whatever made ya place an ad in the paper wi' oor phone number in it?"

I began to explain, "I can't stay here forever and. . ."

"Dinnae interrupt me. Ya should've asked oor permission; the phone line wis engaged fur maest o' the evening, stopping any urgent calls getting through."

It had never occurred to me that I'd need permission to use their number. Would they have allowed it, I wondered. They seemed to want to stifle any sign of independence and ingenuity from the girls in their care. "I'm really sorry for using your number, but how else could they have contacted me?"

"Ya could've used a box number, ya daft lassie," was her reply. *Yes, that's possible, but it would have taken a great deal longer,* I thought, but did not say.

The ad remained in the paper for the next two nights as I had no intention of cancelling it. I sat by the phone waiting to receive the calls. There were six more. The other girls were all very excited and interested in this activity and waited breathlessly in the lounge during each call. They quizzed me intensely after every one, especially if it had been a man. "Did he soond dishy?" "Diz he huv a big hoose?" "Dae ya think he's rich?" and so on . . .

Their imaginations were running riot, wondering what the posts *really* entailed. From my previous experience I wasn't so carried away by the male calls, imagining each one of them to be of a similar disposition to my recent employer. The last call came after the pubs had shut, much to the extreme anger of the woman in charge, who answered it. "It's obscene tae receive a call frae a man at this hour – he's probably drunk," she fumed as she handed me the phone.

She was right – he was exceedingly drunk. He was in a coin box and rambled on at length, in between inserting coins, about my dangerous position. "Ma dear, as yur sae young 'n wi' a bairn, dinnae ya ken that all sorts o' men wi' twisted minds will be contacting ya. They'll be wanting a sleeping companion – ken whit ah mean?" I could almost hear the 'wink, wink and nod, nod' down the line. Naturally I did not need his advice, but when he terminated the call asking if I'd be *his* housekeeper, I laughingly refused. After all his good advice he was no better than the rest.

As I replaced the receiver the woman appeared at her office door and remarked icily, "Ah hope that's the last o' the calls taenight."

Cheerfully I answered, "It probably was," and then went upstairs to bed. My two room-mates were waiting for the latest instalment and we all collapsed in giggles as I told them about the last caller. "Our prison keeper was probably listening behind her office door cos she came out as soon as I'd finished the call."

One of the girls said, "She's probably feeling frustrated wi' all those single men phoning here – she'll be wantin' some o' the action." This set us off again as we imagined the prim and proper spinster with any man at all.

Saturday arrived and I travelled to Edinburgh to meet the most suitable-sounding people. The women that ran the home were none too happy about my expedition, but they reluctantly agreed to me leaving Sean with them for the day, no doubt desperate to witness my rapid departure from their hospitable establishment.

Waverley Station welcomed me again and I looked up at the castle, towering above on its sheer rock face. I was glad to be back. The addresses which I had were in different parts of the city and with the aid of a map and the local buses I set off to the first one. It was a flat in an old tenement building in Leith, near the docks. I didn't like the look of it at all as I trudged up the well-worn, narrow stone steps to the top floor. The door was opened by a middle-aged, big-bellied, balding man. As the majority of callers had been male, I had little choice but to see some of them, in the hope that they'd be either too old or too moral to take advantage of my situation.

The man was pleasant and down to earth – so much so, in fact, that during the interview he openly admitted to needing not only my domestic services but my sexual services as well. "I'm afraid that I can't accept your offer," I said. He acknowledged my refusal without malice and showed me out with no obvious disappointment. No doubt he was clutching at straws and had never really thought that I'd agree to his offer of employment on his terms. Descending the grimy, grey stairs I pondered upon these lonely men who in desperation answered advertisements like mine, in the forlorn hope that a young unmarried mother might be able to fulfil their wildest fantasies.

Despite this first setback I proceeded to the next address on my list, which was on the other side of the city in a run-down area. It was a flat in another gloomy tenement building, again with a single male. This interview, unlike the last, was short but not so sweet. An unkempt, unshaven man in his early thirties opened the door. He took a long look at me, starting at my feet and ending at the last hair on my head. Then he yelled, "No *thank* you," slamming the door in my face. *So, he didn't fancy me, thank goodness.*

With relief I hurried away from that downmarket area to the next address. This was located in a better part of town. It was another tenement, but of higher quality, in a wide, tree-lined street. The stairs were broad, with freshly painted walls and smelt clean from regular scrubbing. My hesitant ring on the polished brass doorbell was answered by a well-dressed, bespectacled young gentleman. He ushered me into a large and luxurious apartment, with high corniced ceilings, from the centre of which hung gleaming crystal chandeliers. Rich oriental carpets adorned the polished wooden floors and expensive-looking antique furniture lined the walls. He introduced me to his wife, who looked as intelligent as her husband and as beautiful as the flat. Their two angelic children, a boy and a girl of primary school age, were summoned. They smiled serenely at me. *This place is at the other extreme – why do they want an unmarried mother as housekeeper and nanny?* My nervousness increased as the interview proceeded, until the wife enquired, "Do you have a driving licence?" Regretfully I replied that I didn't. "That's a pity because we need a chauffeur to take the children to and from school, their extracurricular activities, the shopping and so on." Showing me out they politely hoped that I'd find a suitable position.

Feeling somewhat disappointed I walked to the last address, which wasn't too far away. It was another tenement flat in a busy part of the city and I wearily climbed up a flight of stone steps to the top floor. Anne answered the door. She was plump, with short, black hair and looked in her mid-thirties. "Come in, Margaret. Would you like a cup of tea?"

"Yes, thanks. I've been all over town today without stopping for a drink." We went into the kitchen, which was at the rear of the flat overlooking the back greens of other tenements.

"Sit down and make yourself at home," she said kindly. "I really only need someone to take our daughter to and from primary school. It's just round the corner, but you have to cross a busy road to get to it."

"Well, I could do that easily," I commented, "and I could do the housework and some cooking as well."

"Oh, that wouldn't be necessary – I can manage the cooking and cleaning. I'm a bus conductress and work shifts, so I can't always take Alison to school. I thought it'd be nice for her to have a young baby to play with. She's at a friend's house just now and my husband's at a football match. Do you think you'd be interested?" *This job sounds too good to be true.*

It didn't take long for me to make up my mind. "Yes, I'd be happy to take it," I responded.

"That's great! Let me show you your room. You'll have to share with your son – will that be all right?"

"I'm used to that, although I'll need to find him a cot." The room was large and cosily furnished, with a single bed, armchair, table and chair. There was even a bookcase for my small supply of books.

"I'll keep a lookout for one," she said helpfully. *What a sweet, kind woman.* "When can you start?"

"Next Saturday would be okay, that'll give me time to get organised."

"Good. If you come around lunchtime I'll make sure my husband's in to help you up with your luggage." I left, content that my immediate future was secure and returned happily to Glasgow.

*

I managed to arrive back at the home before the 6pm

curfew and was greeted excitedly by the other girls, who were hungry for all the details of my encounters. Sean had been his usual well-behaved self and was sleeping peacefully. I revelled in the girls' shocked expressions as I told them about my first two interviews. They were pleased that I'd obtained employment and accommodation, but admitted that they'd miss me. "Ye've lightened up oor lives," one of them remarked, "and ye've given us hope that we can also make a life fur oorselves 'n oor weans."

One of the girls, who was only sixteen, had told me she'd fallen pregnant when she'd lost her virginity. "It's nae fair. Ah've ainly hid sex once 'n ah'm up the duff." She was awaiting the birth and, like me, had decided on adoption.

The woman in charge sat behind her large office desk, which gave her an air of authority and looked at me expectantly. "Sae, huv ya managed tae find a suitable position?" I told her my good news and gleefully noted her unconcealed dissatisfaction that I had independently and successfully reorganised my life.

At the beginning of my second week in the home my lawyer notified me that the blood test had been arranged for that Wednesday, at the forensic department of Glasgow University. I dutifully arrived there at the appointed hour, complete with Sean. The doctor and his two assistants were very kind, but this didn't relieve the anxiety I was feeling, knowing that Duncan would be arriving at any moment. They took blood from me first, and this combined with my turbulent thoughts made me feel faint. I sat in the chair feeling icy cold sweat breaking out all over me as I watched them take a sample from Sean. He took it all in his stride, remaining happy and contented, as if having needles stuck into him was no ordeal. This calm acceptance of all the trials and tribulations which he had to endure as a result of being my son, was without doubt our salvation, for if he'd been a troublesome infant I may have been driven to part with him during these early upheavals.

While the doctor and his assistants were busily congratulating me on Sean's good behaviour, laughing and joking to alleviate my feeling of faintness, in strode Duncan, accompanied by a short, mean-looking man, who apparently was his lawyer. I wondered why he'd brought his lawyer with him – maybe they'd thought that the doctor and I were hatching a dark and devious plot involving the mix up of the blood samples. The atmosphere immediately changed from gaiety to cool aloofness as they took Duncan's blood. He was withdrawn, hardly glancing at me and Sean and as soon as he'd given his precious sample he left, his lawyer taking up the rear – *in case of an attack by myself?*

The doctor helped me on with my coat and escorted me to the door. "The result of the test will be ready next week," he informed me. Thankfully I walked away glad that the ordeal was over.

*

Back at the home the girls were all in high spirits as my impending escape became imminent. One of the most pregnant ones had to visit the bathroom at least once a night and knowing this the others, including me, waited until she was safely in bed and then carefully placed an egg outside the bathroom door. Smothering our giggles we retired to bed and were rewarded at 2am by a scream as the poor girl trod on the egg with her bare feet. She burst in on us, irately vowing, "Ah'll get ma ain back on yous, just wait 'n see!" Soon she could also see the funny side and subsided into giggles with the rest of us.

On my last day two of the least pregnant girls suggested going for a lunchtime booze-up as a farewell. "What a good idea," I said, "it's been so long since I've been out, I can hardly remember what it's like." The others were happy to look after Sean again and we set out, clad in our best clothes, accompanied by a liberal splashing of perfume. On reaching the pub we greedily gulped down our drinks, the confinement of the home forgotten as we revelled in our temporary freedom. After several drinks the world took on a rosy aspect and our individual ghastly situations didn't seem nearly as bad. The alcohol had given us an enormous appetite and we found the nearest chip shop, then wandered unsteadily down the street chewing our fish suppers, laughing uproariously at passers-by, who all seemed incredibly dull and sober compared to us.

We arrived back at the home in time for tea and told the others all about our expedition. Afterwards it was my turn to do the washing-up in the huge kitchen in the basement. As I stood at the two large stainless steel sinks, up to my elbows in frothy suds, I became aware that some of the girls were whispering secretly together in a corner, accompanied by a great deal of giggling. *Maybe they're planning something,* I thought vaguely, but forgot about it as we went upstairs to watch TV. The girls sat around in their various stages of pregnancy, some knitting small woollen garments. The mums were busy attending to their babies, who were usually most active in the early evening.

At bedtime my two room-mates were desperately trying to appear as if everything was normal, but they kept sniggering and looking at me. *They must've played a trick on me.* I pulled back my bed covers: a number of large, spiky hair curlers had been carefully placed all over the mattress, underneath the sheet. "Ah, I've caught you," I shouted delightedly and the curlers were removed and redistributed amongst their owners, with much merriment. I climbed into bed and was about to lay my head on the pillow, when I noticed two lumps – one long and thin, the other oval-shaped. Carefully pulling back the pillowslip I found a large sausage and an egg. "Thanks for my breakfast girls," I laughed, which caused even more gaiety, although they were disappointed that I'd discovered them and not squashed them. After all the excitement sleep was a long time arriving, but eventually we were all in the land of dreams.

Twenty-one

In the morning I left the home in a taxi to the railway station, promising to keep in touch with the girls. Back in Edinburgh I took another taxi to my new residence. Anne's husband let me in and took my trunk up the long flights of stairs while I carried Sean. "You can leave your pram at the bottom of the stairs – I'll give you a padlock," he said helpfully. "My name's George, by the way. Anne's on a back shift so she'll not be in 'til about ten."

"Oh, that's okay. Pleased to meet you," I rejoined once I'd got my breath back at the top of the stairs.

"Come away in and make yourself at home. Would you like a cuppa and some lunch?"

"Yes, that'd be great," I replied, aware of my rumbling stomach. I got Sean's lunch ready and was sitting feeding him when Alison appeared. She looked like her dad, with curly brown hair, brown eyes and a sweet smile. "You must be Alison. I'm Margaret and this is Sean."

She stood in the doorway taking it all in. "She's a wee bit shy," George said. "Come and have some lunch, Alison, and say 'hello' to Margaret."

Sitting down at the table by me she almost whispered, "Hello." It wasn't long before her shyness disappeared and she played with Sean after he'd finished eating.

Her dad watched, smiling. "Anne thought she'd love

the baby. We'd have liked another child, but it wasn't to be."

I made sympathetic noises and offered to wash up. "Oh, that's all right. You relax and settle in. Alison'll help me." She obediently began to clear the table and I took Sean into our new room. Anne had found a cot as promised and I happily unpacked my belongings. It felt good to be settled, although I hoped I'd be living in my own flat with a good job in the not too distant future.

The first few days in my new abode passed quickly as I made my room homely and got to know the neighbourhood, which was on the opposite side of town from Matthew's place. I saw little of Anne and George as they were busy working. I took Alison to and from school and after I'd given her a snack she went out to the back green to play with her friends when the weather was fine.

The following week the blood test result came which was as expected, not disproving Duncan's paternity. Over the next weeks I anxiously rang my lawyer on numerous occasions, reversing the charges, until he finally lost his temper. "Margaret, you must be patient and stop phoning me. You'll receive the money in due course." This didn't placate me as I'd already begun to view small flats, some of which were most attractive. I'd also put Sean on a council nursery waiting list, near to where I was staying, which was in a central location. I was becoming increasingly bored and felt that I had to do something towards having a proper career.

One morning, when Anne was on a back shift, we had breakfast together. I badly needed someone to confide in and explained to her that I was hoping for a lump sum settlement with which I'd be able to buy a small flat. She didn't look too pleased. "I see, Margaret. And how long do you think this'll take?"

Oh dear, I shouldn't have told her this. But it was too late. "Oh, it won't be for ages, you know how long lawyers take to do anything," I hurriedly said, hoping that this would pacify her.

"Well, that's all right, I suppose. I don't want Alison to be upset as she's just getting used to you and she really likes Sean." I hadn't realised how her daughter might be affected by our departure and decided not to mention my future plans again.

Then I received a letter from my lawyer. He wrote that Duncan's parents had backed out of their offer of a lump sum settlement and we'd just have to press on with proceedings against him. His theory was that they were hoping I wouldn't sue them after all. The process would take months, during which time I might meet someone else and drop the case. I was bitterly disappointed and angry, but there was little I could do. *I must find a flat to rent instead.* This was no easy task. All the ads for rented accommodation in the paper stated that no children were allowed. I would have to again advertise for a place myself. This time I wrote, *'Wanted, a flat to rent by an unmarried mother and her baby son'.* I used a box number for replies, knowing that Anne wouldn't be too happy if she knew that I was looking for alternative accommodation. I had little hope that there'd be any suitable replies, imagining answers from hordes of unattached men desperate for the services of a young single mum with nowhere to go.

A couple of nights later Anne suddenly burst into my room as I was preparing for bed. She looked extremely angry and demanded, "What've you been up to?" I felt confused and alarmed.

"What do you mean?" I stood in my pyjamas, watching her face grow redder and redder.

"I know you told me that you were waiting for money from Sean's grandparents to buy a flat, but I didn't think you'd be looking for somewhere else to stay behind my back. Then I see this." She flung that night's Evening News at me – my advertisement had been circled in red. "Well, is this your ad?"

I was forced to admit that it was. "You ungrateful hussy! I give you and your son food, shelter and money, and what do I get in return?"

"I'm really sorry," I mumbled.

"Sorry! Is that all you can say?" She glared at me. "I want you out of here first thing tomorrow."

George appeared at the door, just returned from work. "What's going on?" he wanted to know. Anne proceeded to show him the ad, still shaking with rage.

He was much calmer. "If you're happy here, you may stay," he said kindly.

"Thanks, but I'd rather leave after all the nasty things Anne has said."

This set her off again as she shouted, "I can't stand your presence in my home any longer."

George put a comforting arm around her. "Come away to bed. It's late and I'm sure we'll all feel better in the morning." He shot me a sympathetic look as he led her away, sobbing uncontrollably.

*

I shakily got into bed. *What on earth am I going to do?* A picture rose in my mind: I was sitting on my trunk on the pavement, holding Sean in my arms, homeless, jobless and friendless. Then I remembered a place called the Council for the Unmarried Mother and her Child – I would contact them first thing in the morning.

I awoke early, having hardly slept, worrying about my plight and Anne's sudden maniacal hatred of me. Sean was his usual cheery self and I hurriedly fed and changed him, then crept out of the house, not wishing to bump into Anne. I took a taxi to the Council and after a short wait was seen by the organiser. She listened compassionately to my tale of woe, but all she could offer me were yet more housekeeping posts. I flatly refused to take one after my two ghastly experiences, no matter how temporary they might be.

She realised I was adamant then reluctantly admitted, "There's a place for destitute women just along the road from our office. I might be able to get you into it, but it would only be a temporary measure as it's not really appropriate for accommodating babies, or children, for that matter."

I didn't care how unsuitable it was: I just needed a roof over my head. "Oh, that's very kind of you, I'll go there gladly," I responded with relief. We walked along the road to the home and told the lady who ran it about my position.

"You may stay here for around ten days. Hopefully by that time you'll have found more suitable accommodation through your advert." I thanked her profusely and hurried back to the flat, where I breathlessly told Anne that I'd found a place to stay. She said nothing but helped me pack my trunk, bundling my possessions into it at enormous speed, so desperate was she to get rid of me. She breathed heavily, her hands shaking, occasionally glancing at me with stony hatred. I wouldn't have been surprised if she'd attacked me.

There was no sign of George – he must have gone to work. She accompanied us and our luggage to a taxi and we parted without a word. I hoped that I'd never see her again, although I did feel guilty about what I'd done.

It wasn't far to the home and I got out of the taxi, clasping Sean to me, feeling bereft and alone. I hesitantly rang the doorbell and was ushered in by the lady in charge, who exuded an air of efficiency and was dressed in a white starched overall. As we advanced into the hall a number of assorted women gathered, hovering in the shadowy corners, all anxiously peering at the new additions to their habitation. They were an odd-looking bunch, ranging in age from very young to elderly, in various stages of decrepitude, from wild and unkempt to clean and immaculately dressed.

The lady introduced me, "This is Margaret. She's come to stay here for a short time with her baby boy." Encouraged by the greeting they came cautiously nearer and a few of them began to coo over Sean, who rewarded them with a delighted smile. On seeing their overwhelming curiosity in the baby she hurriedly led me upstairs and into my room, shutting the door firmly behind her.

"I should tell you, Margaret, that some of our residents are a little peculiar."

"Yes, I can see that," I replied.

"Well, you saw how curious they were about Sean? Some of them might want to look after him, or take him for a walk in his pram. I'm sure they'd mean him no harm, but they may accidentally hurt him, or, if they took him out they could forget him and leave him somewhere."

"Oh, that sounds awful," I said in alarm.

"You'll need to be extremely careful and not let him out of your sight while you're staying here."

By this time I was praying that I'd find a more suitable place to stay as soon as possible. She continued, "You've been given your own room to safeguard your belongings and the baby. Many of the women are kleptomaniacs and it would be wise to keep your door locked at all times. Don't let any of them into your room, no matter what excuse they dream up to gain entry." *Oh dear, what have I got myself into now?* She noticed my worried face. "Don't worry, I'm only telling you to avoid a worst case scenario. They're actually a sweet, friendly crowd, which I'm sure you'll discover." She then showed me the mattress. "One last thing. You see the mattress is covered by a rubber sheet. This is to protect it from accidents in the night, such as the sudden onset of 'the curse'." With this parting shot she left, wishing me 'a happy stay'.

I breathed a sigh of relief pleased to be left in peace for a while, but it didn't last long. There was a loud knock on my door. One of the older women flashed a welcoming grin at me, exposing a scant number of gold-capped teeth. "Are you settling in okay, dear?" she enquired, her eyes straying past me into the room.

"Yes, thanks," I said firmly, barring the entrance, feeling foolishly unfriendly. *She's just a poor old lady, but I'd better not invite her in.*

"That's good. If you need anything just come to my room – it's number eight down the corridor. I share it with three other girls." I thanked her and watched as she shuffled away, dragging her threadbare slippers along the linoleum floor.

Left alone at last I fell into a deep sleep, along with Sean, who was in his pram beside me. I awoke feeling refreshed and hopeful that suitable answers would come flooding in to my advert. I changed and washed Sean, then took him downstairs to the kitchen to prepare his tea. Most of the women were assembled there, which made me feel rather anxious, but I let one of the more dependable-looking ones dangle him on her knee as I prepared his meal. They all gathered round to watch, eyes popping with wonder, as he swallowed his cereal and sucked gustily at his bottle. It was as if they'd never seen a baby before, especially one in action, and for many of them this was probably true.

After watching his feeding performance, it was their turn to fill their frames with food. One of the staff announced, "Tea's ready," and we all trooped into the adjacent dining room, seating ourselves on either side of a long table, which stretched from end to end of the narrow room, leaving just enough space for the chairs and their occupants. The window was barred, the room being in the basement, giving a partial view of the pavement and the feet of passers-by.

The minister had been invited for tea. He sat at the head of the table, smiling dutifully at us over his gold-rimmed spectacles, his round, clean-shaven face shining with kindliness as he regarded the women. Once we were seated, he closed his eyes, a hush falling over us as he prayed, "For what we are about to receive, may the Lord make us truly thankful."

"Amen," we all murmured in unison. The residents endeavoured to be on their best behaviour, striving not to slop their tea into the chipped saucers. The older ones gallantly chewed on toast spread with home-made raspberry jam, trying not to remove their false teeth to extract the pips lodged painfully behind them. One of the young girls suffered from 'sleeping sickness', I was told, and her neighbour constantly nudged her to keep her awake. She picked bleary-eyed at her food, crumbling the bread into tiny crumbs which she conveyed one at a time through her tired lips.

With their bellies full and their minds brimming with religious benevolence due to the minister's visit, the ladies dutifully cleared the table and washed the dishes, wiping crumbs from their mouths and clothing, complacently burping. Then they retired upstairs to the lounge to watch TV, or doze.

*

The following morning after a disappointing breakfast of tea and toast, I hopefully went to the office of the Evening News. There was only one reply to my ad. It was from a man wanting a housekeeper – *oh no! Not that again.* I was filled with despair. I was still hoping to buy a flat and enquired about the possibility of a loan at an estate agent, but they informed me that at eighteen I was too young to qualify for one, plus I'd need a hefty deposit. The next day there were again no suitable replies to my ad and my despair grew.

I visited the Social Welfare Department who had obtained the disastrous housekeeping post with Matthew, but they were of little help. They did offer to contact my lawyer. "We can ask him to try and persuade Duncan's parents to change their minds about the lump sum," they said, agreeing that the only way I could obtain my own place would be to buy it. Lastly, in desperation I dragged myself and Sean along to the Citizen's Advice Bureau who were most concerned about my situation but could offer no practical assistance.

By this time I was on the verge of tears and fled back to my room where I cried and cried, wondering what to do and wishing that I had the strength to give up my son, for it seemed impossible for me to raise him on my own independently.

Twenty-two

After the third and final night's appearance of my advert there was another reply. I tore open the envelope, praying hard. Spreading out the crumpled letter, I read, *'I have a ground flat in west Edinburgh at a reasonable rent, if you are still interested'.* There followed the address and a contact phone number. My hopes were immediately raised and I phoned and made an appointment to view it.

It was a short bus ride from the city centre, but I could see that it was a less desirable area. I walked down a dismal, dreary street, pushing the pram. The flat was at the rear of a dilapidated tenement block, accessed directly from the uncared for back green. A dowdy-looking, grey-haired woman answered my knock. "Come in, come in," she said, watching my face anxiously. The flat was in a dreadful state. "I'm afraid I made the mistake of letting it to a couple of art students, but there were about ten of them here at the end."

"Ten! How did they all fit in?" I couldn't believe it. There were only two small rooms, a box room, which was used as a coal cellar, and a toilet.

Generously the landlady offered, "You can have the first week rent free – that'll give you a chance to clean the place up and I'll bring some more furniture tomorrow." The main room possessed the only electric socket in the flat and was dominated by an old open range and a double bed. "The range does work," she told me, "it gives out a great heat and you can do your cooking on it." She pointed to a grimy kettle and a couple of saucepans, blackened from the hob. There was a deep stone sink at the window. "The stove heats the water and you can have a wash in the sink," she explained.

Then she showed me the smaller room which was at the end of a short hallway, off of which was the box room-cum-coal cellar. "There's still some coal in there and I'll buy you some kindling," she promised. The smaller room had no electricity – only a gas lamp and a gas fire. It was completely uninhabitable the floor having been largely removed by the previous tenants, presumably to be burnt on the range. Their rubbish had accumulated underneath the few remaining floorboards – coke cans, empty tins, beer bottles and so on. "Don't worry, Margaret. I'll get a new floor laid as soon as possible."

"Oh, good," I said with relief.

She went on, "Once this room's habitable you may find someone else to share with. I've no objection to another baby." *That's great! There must be loads of other unmarried mums desperate like me for their own place. We can babysit for each other too.* I was overjoyed at my good fortune at finding a place of my own at last, even if it did lack many of the luxuries I was accustomed to. I agreed to move in without delay knowing that my benefits would cover the rent until I found a job.

The deal completed I returned to the home in high spirits, clutching my very own front door key. The next day the lady who ran the home drove us to our new residence. She stood looking at the grimy walls, daubed with dubious designs by the previous creative arty inhabitants and suggested: "There's a group of young volunteers at a church in the city centre who might be willing to redecorate it for you." This was a great help and I gratefully thanked her. "Well goodbye, Margaret and good luck in your new abode. I hope it all works out for you and baby Sean," she said as she left.

Once she'd gone I lit the gas cooker oven, which soon warmed up the cold, damp room. Then I ventured out to the shops which were surprisingly cheap and plentiful and purchased food, more kindling and fire-lighters. Back at my flat I prepared and lit a fire in the range, with fingers crossed. To my delight, after some smoke had bellowed into the room, the fire burned furiously, the chimney evidently functioning after its period of neglect. After a while I checked the water. It belched out of the tap an ominously dark orange colour, but eventually settled into an even, colourless flow with which I filled the baby bath, then placed it on the table.

"Look, Sean – it's your first bath in your new home," I said as I plunged him into it. He laughed gleefully and splashed among the soap suds as I washed his firm, plump little body. Clean and content he was soon sleeping peacefully in his pram top which he was rapidly outgrowing, his head pressing against the end of it. As he slept I scrubbed the floor, cleaned the carpet and finally polished the furniture – the room looked almost luxurious in the lamp light. Then exhausted, I fell asleep in the hard but comfortable double bed, cocooned in clean sheets and blankets which the lady from the home had kindly given me.

I woke up in the morning to the sun shining through the cracks on either side of the brown paper blind at the window. I lay luxuriating in the bed's warmth, filled with happiness as I realised that at last I was independent, apart from having a landlady to consider.

There was a council nursery about twenty minutes walk from the flat and I transferred Sean's name to their waiting list. "Our waiting list is very long," they told me, "but a vacancy could arise at any time." With this in mind I scanned the paper every day for suitable jobs.

As promised my landlady soon got the floor fixed and a carpet laid down in the other room. It looked quite homely so I placed yet another advertisement in the Evening News, for an unmarried mother to share with me. I envisaged being deluged with replies from girls as desperate as I had been, but was disappointed to only receive two answers. The first applicant was separated with two babies of five and twenty months old. When she saw the flat she reluctantly agreed with me that it was too small to house three babies. She was also in constant dread that her husband, who was violent, would discover her whereabouts, which discouraged me from pressing her to move in. This was before the days of Women's Aid refuges.

The other person had a baby girl of just two months old. "I'm Christine and this is Katie," she said, looking lovingly at the tiny child in her arms. We sat her beside Sean in the big, threadbare armchair to take a photo, Sean enormous in comparison. She told me her background. "Katie's dad's married with no children. I'm waiting for his divorce to come through and then we'll get married."

"Oh, I see – so you won't be here long."

"He's only just begun proceedings. It could take at least a year, worse luck."

"That's too bad. Do you see much of him?"

She shook her head. "No, not enough. He lives in the north of England and is away a lot in the Merchant Navy." She told me that her family and friends were all in the Scottish borders and had disowned her when she fell pregnant. "That's why I came to Edinburgh, but I'm so lonely." She looked sorrowfully at me through her glasses.

Sympathetically I replied, "I've got no-one here either so it'd be great to have a flatmate and maybe we could babysit for each other, especially in the evenings when they're asleep." She agreed with me and we decided that she would move in the following weekend.

*

This cheered me up tremendously. My life was improving in every way. I'd been offered a post as a technician at a local food research laboratory, despite the fact that I'd told them I was bringing up a baby by myself. Coincidently a vacancy arose at the nursery – it was all falling into place. I had a month of leisure to enjoy before the job started.

The group of young volunteers from the church came and painted the flat soon after my new flatmates moved in. There were about ten of them and they finished in a couple of evenings, slapping white emulsion onto the walls. It transformed the place and we also enjoyed their company which livened up our lives temporarily.

As for the court case, it continued to drag on with little progress being made. The glorious summer weather took my mind off it and I bought two minute mini-dresses to show off my tanned legs. Much of my time was spent sunbathing in the local park while Sean sat next to me on the grass picking at the daisies and dirt with an equal amount of youthful curiosity. He had begun teething, one side of his face burning but it didn't seem to bother him. The sun gave him a lovely tan and he was constantly admired in the street, always rewarding his admirers with his gorgeous smile. It was then that I fully realised how glad I was to have kept him and despite our earlier struggles and disappointments we were at last making a success of our life together.

Christine's parents came for a reconciliatory visit to their new grand-daughter, their hearts melting when they saw her, welcoming her into their family. They weren't too impressed with our home and brought me an old cot for Sean. It was rather rickety but he enjoyed tugging at the bars, trying to stand up, eventually giving up as his wobbly legs gave way and he collapsed onto the mattress with a thud, surrounded by the few toys which he possessed.

*

Our month of leisure rushed by. It was the first day of my new job and anxious to arrive punctually I rose at six, quickly breakfasting with Sean, who probably was wondering what the sudden haste was for. I strapped him into his pushchair and reached the nursery at eight, just as it was opening. I was the first mother to arrive and a nurse told me to put Sean in a playpen at the window. I whispered words of comfort in his ear as I lowered him into the playpen with a heavy heart. He watched me go with large, solemn eyes. It was so hard to leave him there all alone, and as I passed the window on the way out I saw him staring at me with the same serious expression. Overcome with guilt I walked quickly away, trying to forget the painful image of his wee face at the window, attempting to focus instead on my first day as a working mum.

My place of employment, although situated not far from the city centre was difficult to get to without my own transport. I had another twenty-minute walk from the nursery to the bus stop, followed by an anxious wait, then a ten-minute walk from the place where I alighted from the bus to the laboratory. The whole journey from my flat to work via the nursery took over an hour and by the time I arrived I felt tired. At the end of the day it was worse. The nursery closed at 6pm and my work finished at five so there was another mad rush. The matron would be waiting for me as I was usually the last to arrive and glared at her watch as I hurried up the path. Sean had settled in well, she told me, but nevertheless I felt a constant sense of guilt at leaving him for so long each day. Weekends and holidays were havens of peace when we could lie in, cosy in our bed and cot, lazily contemplating the day ahead which we could enjoy together.

Despite the difficulty of travelling to and from the laboratory, I found my new working life stimulating. The research work was interesting and also my colleagues, a lively, intelligent group of people. A pre-requisite of the job entailed attending the local technical college one day a week to study for the national certificate examinations. I enjoyed this break from routine and spent most of my evenings studying once Sean was settled for the night.

My new routine was disrupted by the arrival of Katie's father, Pete, for a week's holiday. He was a likeable character in his late twenties, tanned from his naval life, with a great sense of humour. We ate together most evenings, except when I babysat while they went out to a restaurant. It was fun having a man around and I realised how much I missed the close company of the opposite sex. One evening near the end of his stay Pete came up with a suggestion. "I know a lot of guys in the navy, Margaret. Maybe I could fix you up with one of them? We often dock in Leith and he could see you then."

"I appreciate your concern, Pete, but I don't want to be one of his many port girlfriends from around the world."

"We're not all like that. Look at me, I'm faithful to my girl," he said, giving Christine a sexy smile.

"I'm sure that's true, but I'm quite happy with my work and studies," I said confidently. I may have succeeded in deluding him but actually I was beginning to yearn for a boyfriend again.

Once he'd gone I began asking Christine to babysit on a Friday or Saturday night while I went out to a disco. That first time I invited a pleasant-looking young man back for a coffee. He followed me into my room, took one startled look at Sean asleep in his cot and whispered, "Is that your bairn?"

When I said, "Yes," he muttered something like 'Och, I'm away then,' and almost ran out of the door. You'd think he'd never seen a baby before.

*

After this experience I wasn't too keen on returning to the disco, but ever hopeful I went back on a Saturday night a couple of weeks later. Almost as soon as I entered the room a tall lad with a kind face asked me to dance. We danced for ages and in between numbers I discovered that his name was Mark and he was a year older than me. He seemed to be genuinely interested in me as a person and I told him about my job and mentioned Sean, expecting him to immediately dump me. He didn't. Instead he offered to escort me home and then said, "I'm starving – what about you?"

"Well, yes I am after all that dancing but there'll be nothing open at this time, will there?"

He looked at his watch. "It's 3am but I know a wee café not far from here. Do you fancy going? I'll treat you," he offered. I mistrusted his generosity but my stomach was grumbling with hunger so I accepted. We were too busy eating our pies, chips and beans to talk much and it was a long walk back to my flat. He lived even further away and as it was so late and he'd been so kind, I invited him in. We shared my double bed, for there was nowhere else for him to sleep. Sleep, however, was not what we indulged in, kissing and cuddling until morning, without any actual sex.

The following day he showed no signs of wishing to leave and in fact participated with great pleasure in all the small activities necessary for Sean's little life. While I prepared his breakfast he entertained him, bouncing him on his shoulders and playing 'peek-a-boo'. Sean's delighted squeals woke up Christine and Katie who came through to see what all the noise was about. After I'd introduced them to Mark he said, "Shall I go out and get some rolls and other breakfast stuff?" We didn't have a great supply of food, not having a fridge, so it was agreed that he could buy whatever he fancied.

While he was gone Christine quizzed me about him and I told her all about the previous night. "He sounds too good to be true," she remarked. He came back laden with eggs, bacon, sausages and mushrooms and proceeded to cook us a full English breakfast which was an unexpected treat. Once we had finished eating we walked to the park together; he was totally relaxed at being seen out with a girl pushing a baby in a pushchair. In the park we sat on a bench while Sean crawled contentedly around.

"He's a great kid," he said and then added, "I'm off on holiday to France with a mate of mine in a few days time."

"Oh, that sounds wonderful. I hope you have a good time," I said, removing a small stone which Sean was intent on swallowing.

"I hope so too, but I don't really want to go now that I've met you," he replied, gazing sadly into my eyes. *This is a bit heavy for goodness sake – we only just met.*

He seemed to be genuinely upset so I tried to lighten the mood. "You'll forget all about me once you're over there eating that yummy French food and drinking the vino."

At the end of the afternoon he went home most reluctantly. He still lived with his parents and had just resigned from his job as a salesman in a gentlemen's outfitters shop because he was bored and disillusioned by it. He came to say goodbye the evening before he left for France and could hardly drag himself away to do his packing. "You'll be back in a week," I said, hoping to cheer him up and giving him a long goodbye kiss.

"He seems completely obsessed with you," my flatmate commented and I couldn't help agreeing with her, sighing with relief when he finally left.

The next Saturday he turned up at my flat: he'd only been away for two days. It was early in the morning and I was still in bed when I heard him knocking on the door. "What on earth are you doing here?" He stood gazing at me, his eyes filled with joy, holding many foreign-looking carrier bags. "Well, you'd better come in, I suppose," I said rather coldly, none too happy at having been woken from my weekend slumbers.

"I'm sorry to have woken you, but I couldn't go home because they're not expecting me," he said, putting his bags on the table.

"So why have you come back so soon?" I bent to pick Sean up as he was keen to get out of his cot. He held out his arms to Mark, gurgling happily.

"Look, he remembers me," he said looking pleased, tickling Sean under his chin and making him chuckle. "I spent all my money – that's why I've come back early. I've bought you lots of presents," he said gleefully, " and some for you, young man," he told Sean, who smiled broadly, seeming to understand.

We spent some time opening all the presents – expensive perfume, chocolates and duty-free alcohol. Christine and Katie came through to see what all the commotion was about. He'd even brought them something. I found his behaviour incomprehensible – he'd obviously spent his money as fast as possible to have an excuse to return to me. It was flattering, but worrying. He persuaded me to let him stay for the week and I reluctantly left him each morning to go to work. He made himself useful and painted Sean's cot a lovely lemon colour with transfers of cute penguins at either end. He also bought us food and cooked a tasty dinner every night, with which we drank a glass of smooth French wine. *I could get used to this,* I thought, but at the same time I was looking forward to his departure. It wasn't possible to study with him there and there was another problem – he seemed to be impotent.

At the end of the week he unwillingly returned home, but he continued to visit several nights a week and stay over at the weekend. We had frequent arguments about his lack of employment. He had little idea of what he wanted to do and each time we met he had a different hair-brained scheme about which career to pursue. Our love life continued to be fraught with frustration. "It's because I'm unsettled, without a job. It'll improve when I find one," he assured me.

One evening he arrived and announced excitedly, " I've been offered a job at the flour mill – isn't that great!" It was a low-paid menial job, but at least it was work, and he showed how happy he was by an unusual display of passionate foreplay. At last I witnessed his first beautiful erection; he paraded it around the room, followed by my admiring gaze. I was so overwhelmed at his achievement that I began to giggle uncontrollably, so that when he tried to use it, it had diminished into nothingness, leaving us both frustrated. I cursed myself for my stupidity and lack of understanding.

Optimism kept us together and soon his excuse for his impotence was that our relationship wasn't stable enough. "Let's get married," he proposed and I agreed. We planned to marry about a year later, when Christine would be settled with Pete, but our sex life did not improve. I began to suffer from repetitive stomach upsets, probably as a result of nervous tension. At New Year we went to my sister's home and told them our news. They were pleased, especially as he was so good with Sean. This was the main reason that I stayed with him. My son was toddling around, getting into all sorts of mischief and it was good to have someone else taking care of him. It was a difficult situation. "Everything will be better once we're married," he repeatedly insisted, but although I felt sorry for him, I was rapidly losing hope that this would ever happen.

The gloominess of the flat was also depressing me. Christine had become convinced that her room was haunted and some nights she was so distressed that she slept with me. My fiancé did nothing to stop this – in fact he agreed with her. "You're right, Christine. Your room has a terribly cold atmosphere, even when the gas fire's on full blast." It was a freezing winter and I attributed this so-called 'ghost' to the inadequate heating and the dampness of the walls. Both Sean and Katie had developed chronic coughs as a result.

One night Mark and Christine forced me to go and lie on her bed in the dark, which I did with a show of great hilarity. Their constant obsessive fear had begun to affect me too. I lay there in the dark for several minutes, shaking all over. It was probably my imagination but I decided that it definitely had a ghostly presence and hurriedly returned to my room, much to their satisfaction.

Twenty-three

Signs of spring were beginning to show – beds of yellow and mauve crocus bloomed in the grassy verges and on the trees buds were bursting open. It was my favourite season and one fine day I received the long awaited, almost forgotten, letter from my lawyer. I read that Duncan's parents, after receiving the writ, had decided to pay me a lump sum of one thousand pounds. I sat stunned, the letter in my hand. *One thousand pounds!* It was a great deal of money and I could at last buy my long dreamed of flat. In return I had to sign a statement saying that I would never contact Duncan or his family again. I considered this a small price to pay, despite still having feelings for him.

It didn't take long to find a suitable place, for I fell in love with one instantly, situated in a quiet street near a large park. It was a tiny attic flat with attractively sloping ceilings and comprised two rooms, a kitchen and a toilet. The décor was to my taste, with soothing pale-green walls. I ordered fitted carpets with some of the money left over after the lawyer's fees were settled. The day of entry arrived and I happily left my rented abode, promising to keep in touch with Christine, who moved out to be with Pete soon after.

My change of address had coincided with a change of job. The company running the food research laboratory had been taken over by a large bakery and we were all made redundant. Although this was upsetting it wasn't such a calamity as there were many vacancies in the scientific field. I quickly found a position as a laboratory research assistant at the University of Edinburgh and my new flat was a short bus ride from it.

I collected the keys from the lawyer, full of excitement, and happily ran up the stairs to my very own front door. The carpets were laid in the morning and as soon as the fitters had left I sat down and rolled about on them in delirious joy, inhaling the heady smell of new wool. Whenever I smell a new carpet I remember that first time burying my nose in the fragrance in my own home. Sean seemed equally enchanted with his new abode, crawling about merrily on the warm wool, the sun shining in the large bay windows.

In the afternoon the furniture was delivered, most of which I had bought cheaply at the auction rooms, except for the bed, which was new. There was an important item missing – the cooker. "What's happened to the gas cooker?" I asked the two delivery men.

The older one, who was overweight and out of breath after hauling the furniture up the narrow stairs, replied, "Sorry, but it seems to have been mislaid, lass. We'll deliver it later this evening – dinnae worry." Luckily I had a supply of cooked food in my fridge – another new luxury. In the lounge was a dark alcove and I erected Sean's cot there. He approved of this, chattering incomprehensible but joyous-sounding words.

Much later, after the pubs had shut, the two men returned with the cooker and proceeded to connect it, merrily breathing beery fumes and heavily hinting for a tip. "Thanks lass. Good luck in your new home," they said, finally leaving me in peace. Exhausted by the day's excitement and activity, I fell into my new bed and was asleep immediately.

*

It had been agreed that Mark would come and live with us; he arrived the next morning, a Saturday, with his belongings. "What a great wee place, Margaret," he said, "it's nice to have our own bedroom too." The lack of a bathroom didn't bother him too much. He often went home for a bath, sometimes sneaking me in when his folks were out, or we would go swimming and have a shower afterwards.

He had recently joined the police force and at least looked like a 'new man' in his smart uniform. He hadn't told them that he had changed his address, fearing that it might jeopardise his career if they knew he was living with me. Several mornings when he was on early shift, he overslept. I had to drag myself down the road to the phone box and, attempting to sound like his mother, say something like, "I'm afraid Mark won't be able to come to work today as he has a heavy cold," or similar excuses. Eventually they became suspicious at these not very convincing calls, and contacted his mother who told them he was living with me and gave them my address. I had no knowledge of this until one morning around 8am, after another apology phone call, there was a loud knock on the door. I was shocked to see two large and imposing uniformed police officers, who insisted on entering my flat, much to my dismay. They burst in on my fiancé, languishing in bed, and the senior one said, "If you don't terminate your 'living in sin' with this woman, you'll have to leave the police force."

Mark sat straight up in bed and shouted, "I've got no intention of moving out." After they had gone I tried to persuade him to go home as I didn't want to wreck his career, but he refused. He did however tentatively suggest that we get married earlier. I was uncertain about this as our sex life had hardly improved and I wasn't sure that I even loved him enough. It was such a pity as he was so good with Sean, taking him walking in the park, picking him up and carrying him on his shoulders when his little legs could go no further. The police were as good as their word and it wasn't long before he was jobless again. Our sex life became non-existent and we frequently argued, increasing my feeling of frustration.

I had been increasingly thinking about Duncan as my relationship with Mark deteriorated and in desperation one evening I went along the road in the pouring rain to the phone box. With crossed fingers and a pounding heart I dialled Duncan's number. Miraculously he answered. I told him I was missing him terribly and begged him to come and see me, swallowing my pride in huge chunks, completely forgetting about the paper I had signed. To my amazement he said he would come and we arranged to meet at the train station the following Saturday.

On my return to the flat I told Mark, uncertain of his reaction. "Oh, Margaret, it's good that he's coming to see you and Sean. I'm looking forward to meeting him." *I can't believe he means this – it's the height of reasonableness.* He sat gazing fondly at me and I realised that he loved me but I still loved Duncan.

With a heavy heart I made my way to the station – I hadn't had the courage to tell Duncan about Mark. He was waiting near the entrance in his car and looked apprehensively at me as I got in, becoming even more nervous when I told him about my relationship. "Why didnae you tell me aboot this guy? I widnae hae come if ah'd kenned aboot him," he said angrily, clutching the wheel, ashen-faced.

"Oh Duncan, please come to tea now you're here. Mark's looking forward to meeting you. I promise you he's not violent." He refused several times but finally relented, driving aggressively through the Saturday afternoon traffic to my home, insisting repeatedly that he would leave immediately after tea, wondering aloud why on earth he had come to see me at all.

I gritted my teeth, hoping that the evening would improve after his belly was full with my appetising roast chicken and vegetables, which I had prepared that morning. He parked outside the flat, cautiously looking up at the windows, expecting what – a sniper maybe? Mark answered the door cordially, inviting him in and producing cans of beer, which had a noticeably beneficial effect on his behaviour. He sat supping at his can, looking around my small lounge with a more relaxed expression on his face. Then his gaze fell upon the child in his cot in the alcove. He had been playing with his toys but when he saw his father looking at him he hauled himself up, wanting to get out. Duncan regarded his son over the rim of his can, his face now agitated. More cans were consumed by him and then Mark lifted Sean from his cot. He delightedly made his way around the room, hanging on to the furniture, showing off mercilessly to the visitor. Despite himself, Duncan was forced to watch his cheerful antics, and even began to laugh at the funny faces Sean was making, rolling his eyes merrily at his father, completely unaware of their relationship.

I took Sean into the kitchen to have his tea, leaving the men to resume their conversation about football as they tucked into their dinner. The relief on Duncan's face at his removal was obvious to me, but I fondly thought that he was experiencing emotional turmoil at seeing his son again, so changed, being quite a little boy already. As I washed the dishes I began to fantasise about the outcome of the evening. Duncan would declare his undying love for me and his son, while Mark, sadly, but with a sense of what was right, would relinquish his hold on me.

My fantasies were rudely interrupted by Mark's entrance into the kitchen. "Margaret, would you mind if I took Duncan along the road for a quick pint?"

"No, that's fine Mark," I answered, "as long as you're not too long." *A visit to the pub would mellow Duncan considerably,* I decided.

Looking very pleased with themselves they left, hardly bothering to say goodbye. I put Sean to bed and read him some of his favourite stories, then settled down to listen to some records for an hour or so. I began looking at my watch, my anger gradually mounting as the minutes ticked by with no sign of my men. *You're a fool to have ever become involved with either of them – they're both completely useless!* Eventually, long after closing time, they returned making a great deal of noise on the stair. It was immediately apparent that they were both extremely drunk as they staggered through the door. I greeted them with a stony face and began brewing up black coffee, which they insisted that they did not want.

They were so jovial that I couldn't stay angry for long and began laughing and joking with them. We finally ran out of conversation and decided it was bedtime. I made up the settee in the lounge for Duncan and retired to my bedroom with Mark. I was feeling very romantic, wanting to be held in Duncan's arms once more, and lay in bed wishing I was in the lounge. Soon Mark was breathing heavily in a drunken stupor and I wondered if I dare sneak through to the other room. Frustration and lust got the better of me and I crept from the room with bated breath. My fiancé didn't stir.

Duncan, being a hardened drinker, was in no such state. He was still awake, no doubt thinking about the evening's events. He showed little surprise when I appeared and gladly welcomed me onto the settee, where we made love without further ado. I still remained unsatisfied, however, for my turbulent thoughts wouldn't allow me to relax and enjoy this long awaited moment. We tried to discuss the situation, as I peered at him through the semi-darkness, attempting to read the expression in his eyes. What he said pierced my heart. "Margaret, I dinnae want tae marry you – I'd make an awfy husband. You should marry Mark, he obviously cares aboot ya 'n he's great wi' Sean," he repeated several times. How he could be so sure about this I could not imagine, and then realised that he was simply making the situation easy on himself (as well as being honest). I got up, wandered into the kitchen and gazed out at the starlit sky, feeling miserably empty. I considered jumping out of the window to ease my pain, becoming colder and colder, hoping that he would come through and comfort me. He never did. In despair I returned to the warmth of my bed, where Mark was sleeping peacefully. I lay staring blankly at the ceiling, my mind numb with misery.

I awoke early to the sound of the front door being carefully shut, followed by the soft, stealthy tread of retreating footsteps. I leapt out of bed and dashed into the lounge – it was deserted, except for my son who had just woken up, unaware of his father's flight. I lifted him up, cuddling him close and smelling his warm, heavenly smell, my love for him a balm to my pain. My fiancé came through, nursing his hangover. "Where's Duncan?" he asked, surprised at the empty settee.

"He must've left early," I replied. Mark looked at me with concern and then made a big fuss of me, preparing our breakfast, not asking any difficult questions. He was especially tender in his affections for several weeks, no doubt realising that the competition had been removed. Our sex life, however, did not improve and I became increasingly irritated by his presence and his constant suggestion that marriage would solve all our problems. *I didn't want to marry him.* Finally I told him. He didn't take it well and after he had left he still pestered me, waiting outside my work to speak to me, trying to persuade me to take him back. I pitied him, but there was little that I could do.

Twenty-four

I decided to look for a larger flat as my salary had increased and I would be able to obtain a mortgage. The plan was to let out one or two rooms to other unmarried mums, to help pay the mortgage and provide babysitting for each other. I was feeling rather lonely after Mark had left and advertised for someone before I moved. There were several replies and I found a girl who I liked immediately. Her name was Veronica, or Ronnie as she liked to be called, and she had an adorable baby girl, Siobhan, who seemed to be in eternal good spirits.

She told me, "I was born in Glasgow but I went to the States to live a few years ago. I met this guy – Steve. He was real handsome and we had a bit of a 'thing' together. Then, stupid me, I fell pregnant. He didn't want to know so I came back here to have my baby. Giving birth in the States is *so* expensive. I didn't realise how difficult it'd be to find somewhere to live though." She gave an easy laugh, her lively grey eyes smiling out of her wide, happy face, which was framed by long, wavy light-brown hair. She then added, "I'm really desperate to get a place. I'm living with my grandmother at the moment and it's pretty cramped. When are you thinking of moving?"

"Well, I haven't found anywhere yet and it'll take a while for the legal stuff to get done," I said, watching her face fall. "I suppose you could move in here temporarily, but there wouldn't be much space either."

"Oh, don't worry! I don't have much stuff and Siobhan's still small enough to sleep in her pram top." She looked at me expectantly.

"Okay, you can have the bedroom and I'll sleep on the settee," I said.

"Wonderful! When can we move in?" She was ecstatic and Siobhan joined in, cooing joyfully.

"Whenever you want." I was becoming as excited as her.

She moved in the following day and we began flat hunting immediately. It wasn't long before we found one that we both loved. It was in a central part of town, not far from my second disastrous housekeeping position, but this did not deter me. The flat was on the first floor of an old stone tenement and was spacious, comprising a lounge, kitchen-cum-dining room, a large and small bedroom, a sizeable box room which could be used as a bedroom and, what luxury – a bathroom! All of this for the princely sum of three thousand pounds! The owners found it hard to believe that I would be able to raise enough money to buy it and were pleasantly surprised when I made the offer, accepting it at once. I went round that evening and celebrated the purchase with them. "You'll love it here, Margaret," the husband assured me, "we'll be sad to leave but we have to move nearer my new job in Glasgow." I sat sipping a glass of red wine, hardly able to comprehend that this lovely place was all mine at the tender age of twenty.

*

I soon sold my flat, which had increased in value significantly after just one year. The removal day dawned bright and sunny, which was a blessing as Ronnie and I carried all the items we could manage downstairs to the tiny front garden. I had arranged a small company, who charged by the hour, and we sat waiting impatiently for their van, while Sean ran around excitedly and Siobhan sat on Ronnie's knee, gurgling contentedly while watching his antics. The two removal men arrived and surveyed the scene with amusement. "My, you've been busy, girls! Is there anything left for us to do?" the older one enquired. They soon had the large pieces of furniture and our belongings from the front garden in the van and in we all clambered. The whole move only took a couple of hours, much to my delight as I needed money to buy extra furniture. Once the men had gone Ronnie and I wandered from room to room, marvelling at the spaciousness, while we waited for the water to heat up for our very first bath.

I had transferred poor Sean to yet another nursery close to the flat. My work at the University of Edinburgh was a short stroll away, through a beautiful tree-filled park. A return visit to the auction rooms furnished the flat so I advertised for another flatmate. Ronnie and I chose a girl, Doreen, of around our age who had a two-year-old daughter called Rosie – she would be a playmate for Sean, I thought, as they were around the same age.

Unfortunately the old saying of 'two's company, three's a crowd' proved to be true, for soon after she moved in, trouble began. There were constant rows over who should bath first: the hot water tended to run out once the second bath was drawn, and if we all wanted a bath the same evening the third person had to wait too long. Another problem was the washing-up. We were supposed to take it in turns to do the dishes and clean the communal areas but Ronnie, who didn't work, did the breakfast dishes only. Doreen and I would return after a long day's work, to mountains of dirty crockery and after we had all eaten we argued about who's turn it was to wash them. Then there was Rosie. She shared the box room with Sean and was constantly fighting with him, staying awake far longer than him and disturbing my studies as my room, the lounge, was next door. I was now studying for the Higher National Certificate and what with Rosie's noisy tantrums and Ronnie's loud record player, I couldn't find much peace in the evenings.

This arrangement which initially had seemed such a good idea, both financially and socially, was proving to be less of a success than I had expected. We did have some good nights out together despite our disagreements, until one weekend when I went by myself to a college Halloween party. It had been organised by a particularly attractive young man in my class. All the girls were in hot pursuit of him – the main reason we attended his party. I had made a special effort with my appearance, wearing a high-necked, dusky-pink blouse with ruffled sleeves and a maroon woollen midi-skirt with black tights and black leather knee-length boots, the height of fashion then. I now wore my hair longer, trying to tame the waves into sleek straightness, applying rouge to my cheeks, the pale look having gone out of style.

My classmate lived in a basement flat and he had dimmed the lights, making it difficult to see in the gloom. The first thing I noticed was the lack of alcoholic refreshment – I should have brought a bottle of something. An older man in my class, Alastair, beckoned me over to where he was sitting. "Hi, Margaret. I didn't know you were coming to this. May I offer you some whisky?" I never drank the stuff – it was too strong and I disliked its taste, but there was nothing else on offer so I accepted. He poured some into a paper cup and I gulped it down, unable to see how much he had given me in the darkened room. "Would you like some more?" he offered, topping up my cup. Alastair was a tall, thin unattractive man with receding hair, married with three children and I soon realised with dismay that he was flirting with me. No doubt this was the reason he had been plying me with whisky.

I moved away from him and saw one of my girlfriends beckoning from the other side of the room. "I'm going to speak to Sally," I told him, glad of the chance to escape.

"So, you've managed to get away from Alastair," she chuckled, "he's such a lech."

"You're right," I responded. "He's been trying to get me drunk with his whisky and I think he's succeeded."

"I thought you weren't too steady on your feet," Sally laughed. Then she pointed out another classmate. "You see that guy over there?"

"Hmm, yes. What about him?" I was trying to focus, hardly recognising him through the gloom.

"Well, I think Dave and you would be great together," she enthused. I had hardly noticed him at college but had seen him in the Co-op at the end of my street on several Saturdays, doing his shopping. One Saturday Sean had run off pushing our trolley, colliding with Dave who was standing pondering packets of curry powder.

"Is this your wee brother?" he'd asked. I was embarrassed, muttered something unintelligible and disappeared as fast as I could, blushing furiously. I had told nobody at college, except Sally, about Sean, still aware of the stigma attached to unmarried mothers.

"I'm not sure that I like him and he's seen me with Sean in the supermarket," I told Sally.

"Go on, give it a try. I think he'd make a great Dad," she urged.

I sat in a haze of whisky and watched as Sally took control. She strode over to Dave and whispered something in his ear. The next thing I knew he was asking me to dance. It wasn't long until the whisky forced me to retire to the bathroom, where I was violently ill. Eventually I emerged to a long queue of students, who had been desperately thumping on the door. My dancing partner was waiting patiently outside and he lead me to a bedroom where I collapsed on the bed, while he read biochemistry text books at my side. From time to time Sally popped her head round the door. "Just checking that he's not molesting you," she quipped.

Once I was sufficiently recovered he drove me home, but the motion of the car caused me to vomit the remaining contents of my stomach out of the window. *When had I done that before?* Undaunted by my disgusting behaviour he asked me to go to a music concert with him the following night. I accepted, grateful for his kindness.

*

Sally's matchmaking proved to be a success. Dave and I soon became close and he was indeed great with Sean, without Mark's problems. He also worked in the scientific field and we began studying together in the evenings. Just before Christmas he moved in with me, but not for long. On Christmas day we went to his parents' house for dinner. Just before the meal they summoned him into another room, where they had a row about us cohabiting. "If you want to marry, that's fine, but you'll get married from *our* house," his father shouted. My poor boyfriend came through to tell me the news. We were too upset to stay and he drove us home, without having had our Christmas dinner.

Once back at my flat he consoled me but said, "I'm sorry Margaret but I'll need to go home. I don't want to fall out with my folks. We can still see a lot of each other and I'll stay over at weekends like before." With that he packed up the few things that he had brought and went home, leaving me alone with Sean as my flatmates were away visiting their families. It was my worst ever Christmas.

At New Year we visited my sister and her husband. My mum and 'Big Jim' were also there and fell in love with their grandson, everything forgiven. They all liked Dave and often took Sean out for a walk, giving us precious time alone. One evening they babysat while we went out for a meal. It was then that we decided to marry in the summer to the delight of all my family.

Back in Edinburgh I broke the news to Ronnie and Doreen. They were pleased for us but had to start planning where they were going to live as Dave would move in with me. It all worked out well. Doreen was allocated a council flat while Ronnie became reunited with Siobhan's dad, which meant that she moved back to the States to live. We kept in touch and years later Sean had a brief fling with Siobhan when he visited her in California! Dave and I produced a sister, Sarah, for Sean just over a year after we married and we moved out of Edinburgh, near to where his parents lived, to be in the countryside.

Epilogue

The years passed and from time to time Sean would ask me about his real father. I could only tell him what I knew as I lost touch with him after his disastrous visit. Then, after fifteen years, my marriage broke up and Sean began to think increasingly about Duncan.

He married a Canadian and moved to Canada some years after the break-up and when he was forty-two he asked me to try and find his dad. With the help of the charity Birthlink we discovered that Duncan had married and moved to Edinburgh, where they had a son and a daughter, who was born about a year after Sarah. Sadly Duncan died young – when he was only thirty-five. His wife remarried and later, as she was Canadian, she moved back to Canada with her family. The son and daughter remained in Canada, married and produced six children between them. Sean contacted them by email (which he'd been given by Birthlink) and they all met up, including Sean's daughter, Olivia, despite living some distance from each other. Although Sean was sad not to have met his dad he now has two half-siblings and six half-nephews and nieces – and all living in the same country as him!

References

Wiktionary – Appendix: Glossary of Scottish slang and jargon

Glesga Glossary – Glesga Ned Cartoon

Acknowledgements

I would like to thank my family, especially my sister, Jean, for assistance with editing and my son, Sean and daughter, Sarah, for their support.

Printed in Great Britain
by Amazon